FINANCING INDEPENDENT FILMS:

50 Ways to Get the Golden Goose, Not a Goose Egg
Volume 1, Film Financing Series
2nd Edition

M. M. Le Blanc, JD, MBA
Veteran Hollywood Studio Executive * Film Finance Entertainment Attorney

FINANCING INDEPENDENT FILMS:
50 WAYS TO GET THE GOLDEN GOOSE,
NOT A GOOSE EGG
Volume 1, Film Financing Series
2nd Edition

©2018, 2021 BizEntine Press
Cover Design: ©2018, 2021 BizEntine Press

Print ISBN: 978-1-947471-27-6
epub ISBN: 978-1-947471-34-4
mobi ISBN: 978-1-947471-35-1

All rights reserved.

No part of this book may be copied, duplicated, translated, reproduced, disseminated, transmitted, stored, archived, retrieved, or otherwise used in any manner and in any media now known or hereafter devised without the publisher's prior written authorization.

Manufactured in the United States of America by

For everyone who wants to raise money and make movies.

Paris ne s'est pas faite en un jour !
Merci, St. Gabriel.

BOOKS by M. M. Le BLANC

Entertainment Industry Series
Vol. 1, ©HEAP PROTECTION: COPYRIGHT HANDBOOK FOR FILMS
Vol. 2, ©HEAP PROTECTION: COPYRIGHT HANDBOOK FOR SCREENPLAYS
Vol. 3, ©HEAP PROTECTION: COPYRIGHT HANDBOOK FOR TELEPLAYS
Vol. 4, ©HEAP PROTECTION: COPYRIGHT HANDBOOK FOR TV PROJECTS
Vol. 5, CHEAP ®ROTECTION: COPYRIGHT HANDBOOK FOR MUSIC
Vol. 6, ©HEAP PROTECTION: COPYRIGHT HANDBOOK FOR LITERARY WORKS

Film Financing Series
Vol. 1, FINANCING INDEPENDENT FILMS: 50 WAYS TO GET THE GOLDEN GOOSE, NOT A GOOSE EGG
Vol. 2, FILM EQUITY CROWDFUNDING: 10 LEGAL WAYS TO SELL EQUITY IN YOUR FILM

Award-Winning Fiction

EVANGELINE: PARADISE STOLEN, Vols. I & II, 1st Ed.
EVANGELINE: PARADISE STOLEN, Vols. I & II, 2nd Ed.
EVANGELINE: PARADISE STOLEN, Vol. I, 3rd Ed.
EVANGELINE: PARADISE STOLEN, Vol. II, 3rd Ed.
EVANGELINE: PARADISE STOLEN, Vols. I & II eBook
EVANGELINE: PARADISE STOLEN, Vol. III
THE PITCHER'S PRAYER, a Novel of Faith, Family the First Amendment and...Baseball

Award-Winning Non-Fiction
ACADIE THEN AND NOW, Collective Author,
L'ACADIE HIER ET AUJOURD'HUI, Collective Editor
THE ACADIAN MIRACLE, 50th Anniversary Ed.
THE ACADIAN MIRACLE, 53rd Anniversary Ed. with Index
THE TRUE STORY OF THE ACADIANS, 90th Ann. Ed.
THE TRUE STORY OF THE ACADIANS, 93rd Ann. Ed. with Index

ENTERTAINMENT & LEGAL "HOW-TO" BUSINESS BOOKS
Published by

 *Entertainment Industry Series*

Vol. 1, ©HEAP PROTECTION:
COPYRIGHT HANDBOOK for FILMS

Vol. 2, ©HEAP PROTECTION:
COPYRIGHT HANDBOOK for SCREENPLAYS

Vol. 3, ©HEAP PROTECTION:
COPYRIGHT HANDBOOK for TELEPLAYS

Vol. 4, ©HEAP PROTECTION:
COPYRIGHT HANDBOOK for TV PROJECTS

Vol. 5, CHEAP ℗ROTECTION:
COPYRIGHT HANDBOOK for MUSIC

Vol. 6, ©HEAP PROTECTION:
COPYRIGHT HANDBOOK for LITERARY WORKS

Film Financing Series

Vol. 1, FINANCING INDEPENDENT FILMS:
50 WAYS TO GET THE GOLDEN GOOSE,
NOT A GOOSE EGG

Vol. 2, FILM EQUITY CROWDFUNDING: 10 LEGAL
WAYS TO SELL EQUITY IN YOUR FILM

CONTENTS

BOOKS BY M. M. Le BLANC   4

BIZENTINE "HOW-TO" BUSINESS BOOKS   5

I: FILM FINANCE OVERVIEW: 9
What It's All About
1. Executive Overview   11

II: GETTING STARTED: 17
Set Up for Success
2. Choose a Business Entity   19
3. Hire an Entertainment Attorney   29
4. Acquire Literary Material Rights   37
5. Copyright Your Work   47
6. Use Alternative Dispute Resolution   53
7. Hire Film Marketing Professionals   59

III: GETTING THE BUDGET: 69
Count 'em, 50 Ways
8. The 50 Ways   71
9. WAYS 1-7: Skin in the Game   74
10. WAYS 8-15: Donations & Grants   85
11. WAYS 16-22: Products & Services   103
12. WAYS 23-28: Team Effort   115
13. WAYS 29-30: Locations   125
14. WAYS 31-34: Soft Money 1: Rebates & Incentives   129
15. WAYS 35-36: Soft Money 2: Tax Credits   135
16. WAYS 37-38: Pre-Sales   140
17. WAYS 39-46: Debt   146
18. WAYS 47-50: Equity Securities   163

IV: MONEY, MONEY, MONEY: 183
Where It All Goes
   19. The Waterfall 185

V: DISTRIBUTION & BEYOND: 193
Get Your Film Out There
   20. Distribution 195
   21. Chain of Title & Deliverables 205
   22. What's Next? 211

INDEX 215

APPENDIX: 219
A. Entertainment Associations, Guilds &
   Organizations 219
B. Film Publications, Blogs & Websites 220
C. Grant Resources 222
D. U.S. Government Offices 223
E. State Secretary of State or Economic
   Development Offices 223

FORMS BANK: 225
A. Film Financing Checklist 225
B. Sample Chain of Title 228

ABOUT THE AUTHOR 230

CONTACT THE AUTHOR 231

CONTACT THE PUBLISHER 231

NOTES 232

I

FILM FINANCING OVERVIEW

What It's All About

1.

EXECUTIVE OVERVIEW

So, you want to produce an independent film. Maybe it will be your first. Or you have produced for others and now want to make your own film. Or you are a seasoned producer on the look-out for additional financing sources for upcoming film projects.

No matter the reason, you have found the right book. It is true that *FINANCING INDEPENDENT FILMS* does actually provide *50 WAYS TO GET THE GOLDEN GOOSE, NOT A GOOSE EGG*. But it also goes beyond the 50 Ways to include many other topics, as summarized in this Chapter.

The objective of this book is twofold:
- To provide multiple Ways to raise film financing and reduce the budget; and,
- To outline a sequence of activities crucial to filmmaking success, which can translate into greater revenues and actual profits to the owners.

However, this book differs greatly from other film financing books. The primary difference is that it was written specifically for non-lawyer producers, directors, filmmakers, film students, educators and all others interested in learning the 50 Ways to obtain film financing for independent feature films.

This book also goes above and beyond just offering numerous sources of potential film financing. It explains in *non-legalese* plain English how to use these sources not only to raise financing but also to lower film budgets.

A financial rule of thumb is that profit derives only from generating greater revenues or reducing budgeted costs. This book takes the double-edged approach to both ends of a film budget -- raising the financing and reducing the budget to require less financing.

You may be surprised to learn that buying a film equity interest is a "security" subject to federal and state securities laws. To sell equity interests in a film, producers must either file public registration statements or be exempt therefrom. This book includes some of these exemptions, but the author gives more in the upcoming *FILM EQUITY CROWDFUNDING: 10 LEGAL WAYS TO SELL EQUITY IN YOUR FILM,* Volume 2 of the *Film Financing Series.*

CAVEAT

PLEASE NOTE: This book, *FINANCING INDEPENDENT FILMS: 50 WAYS TO GET*

THE GOLDEN GOOSE, NOT A GOOSE EGG, provides general information solely for informative and educational purposes, and is not legal advice. It is always recommended to consult qualified legal counsel on specific issues relating to film financing, debt, equity, securities and other such subjects.

ORGANIZATION OF THIS BOOK

This book is organized into 5 Parts which are divided into 22 concise, easy-to-read Chapters. In the back of the book are the Index and bonus material -- an Appendix with pages of resources, and a Forms Bank with a Film Financing Checklist and sample Chain of Title.

A reader could skip around Chapters in this book since each is written independently. But it is highly recommended to read the Chapters in order. The book begins with general film financing and production information then delves into more specific details on the 50 Ways in subsequent Chapters.

This book is particularly useful for understanding that raising film financing for an independent film is ultimately in the hands of its producer or filmmaker. The tools provided can contribute to budgetary success.

BUILD YOUR WEALTH IN THE INDUSTRY

The basis of all wealth in the entertainment industry is Intellectual Property. Once a producer, director or filmmaker options, acquires or writes the screenplay for a film, she needs to obtain substantial funding for more development and for production and post-production to create the IP of a film.

This book provides 50 Ways to make the budget to produce a film or to reduce the budget, resulting in the need for less funding.

Exploiting the rights to a produced film is an expensive endeavor. Marketing, promoting, film festival entries, travel, screenings, Prints & Advertising ("P&A"), public relations and other costs take substantial time and money.

The age-old conundrum for producers has always been how to get the money it takes to make the money they need to make the film they want to make the profit they desire in order to start the process all over again.

This book aims to solve that enigma with multiple solutions. Readers obtain a variety of means at their fingertips to decide which individual method or combination of methods will work best for them.

This book is the solution for producers and filmmakers to make or reduce their budget, using the methods and tools discussed herein.

CHAPTER SUMMARIES

The Chapters in this book describe 50 different Ways to fund an indie film budget. These include how to raise funding or lower the budget, as well as many other valuable tools for producers, directors, filmmakers, film students and educators.

In Part I, Chapter 1 provides an Overview of the book and information in the Chapters.

In Part II, Chapter 2 details different types of business entities and how to choose the right one for you. Chapter 3 discusses questions to ask when determining whether to hire an entertainment attorney for your production, and if so, who is the best fit. Chapter 4 describes important agreements used to option and acquire literary material like screenplays and rights to adapt books for films. Chapter 5 covers the importance of copyrighting, when copyright attaches to your work and how to copyright a film and a screenplay. Chapter 6 summarizes methods of alternative dispute resolution, like mediation and arbitration, in lieu of litigation. Chapter 7 describes industry professionals who assist producers to market their films.

In Part III, Chapters 8 through 18 discuss the 50 Ways to raise film financing and reduce the budget. These include skin in the game, grants, donations, products, services, equipment, non-equity crowdfunding, team effort, locations, incentives, soft dollars, debt, equity securities and much, much more. These Ways include securities exemptions from registration of film equity ownership offerings, like the Securities and Exchange Commission new rules for "Regulation Crowdfunding" and a "California Exemption."

16 | EXECUTIVE OVERVIEW

In Part IV, Chapter 19 explains the waterfall. This is the order of repayment of lenders, creditors, investors and back-end participants from film revenues and profits.

In Part V, Chapters 20 through 22 discuss the next steps once a film is completed. Chapter 20 reviews film distribution deals and P&A. Chapter 21 explains the chain of title and deliverables that film buyers require. Chapter 22 offers a road map for producers to move forward and achieve the goal of financing an independent film.

BONUS MATERIALS

Bonus materials that are found in the Appendix and Forms Bank include:
- Entertainment Associations, Guilds and Organizations;
- Film Publications & Online Resources;
- Grant Sources;
- Government Resources;
- State Secretary of State Offices;
- 50 Ways Checklist; and
- Sample Chain of Title.

Be sure to refer to your copy of *FINANCING INDEPENDENT FILMS: 50 WAYS TO GET THE GOLDEN GOOSE NOT A GOOSE EGG* like a manual or handbook as you raise financing.

Start building greater wealth for you and your business in the entertainment industry today by using one or a combination of the 50 Ways. *Happy film financing!*

II

GETTING STARTED

Set Up for Success

2.

CHOOSE A BUSINESS ENTITY

Now that you are in the film-financing mode, it is time to choose the right business entity for operating your production company. If you already own a company, you may wish to consider creating a new "single purpose" production company just for producing your film, for liability purposes.

This Chapter discusses different business entities that can be formed for use as production companies or for single-purpose production companies. These entities may also be used for other entertainment business purposes, such as loanouts to "loan out" your services as a producer, director, writer or other professional.

Producers who wish to remain sole proprietors without creating a separate legal entity can choose to create a fictitious business and operate under a business name, often called a "DBA" or a "Doing Business As" operating structure. The different types of business entities are discussed below.

A. TYPES OF BUSINESS ENTITIES

When choosing a type of business entity within which to operate, the key factors to consider are the producer's personal needs, financial situation, tolerance for risk and arrangement with business partners, if any.

Business entities that are typically used by producers and filmmakers include:
- Corporation, including a Loanout;
- Limited Liability Company;
- Partnership, including General, Limited and Limited Liability Partnerships; and
- Sole Proprietor/Fictitious Business/DBA ("Doing Business As").

Generally, legal entities are filed with the relevant business office of a state. Most states assign this responsibility to a state Secretary of State or to a state business development office where the documents are filed and the legal entities are registered.

The Appendix in the back of this book lists contact information for state Secretary of State offices. A discussion of corporations as legal structures for production companies follows.

1. CORPORATION

A corporation is a legal business entity which is separate and distinct from its owners, called shareholders. They may be individuals, businesses or even corporations. Requirements for formation vary with each state, but many states require a corporation name to end in "Inc.," "Incorporated," "Co." or "Ltd." This distinguishes a corporation from other types of business entities.

Shareholders appoint the directors, who make the management decisions. The directors hire the officers to perform the day-to-day operations, employ staff and make daily operating decisions. Officers and directors are bound to act in the best interests of the company's shareholders.

The positive attributes of a corporation are many. The entity can do almost anything an individual can do legally, such as borrowing or lending money, executing and performing contracts, filing suit and being sued, and owning and disposing of assets and other benefits.

A major benefit of a corporation is its shareholder shield against liability for the corporate debts and other financial responsibilities. If the corporation cannot or does not pay its debts, creditors can look only to corporate assets for repayment, not to the shareholders, except in cases of fraud or illegality.

Two types of corporations are:
- C Corporations; and
- S Corporations.

C corporations are taxed on income at a corporate rate, which may be greater or less than an individual's income tax rate depending on taxable income, deductions and other factors.

A negative aspect of a C corporation is double taxation. The corporation pays corporate income tax on taxable revenues disallowing any deduction for shareholder dividends. And these owners pay a second tax, their personal income tax, on the dividends received. Revised tax laws may reduce, increase or otherwise affect tax rates for individuals and/or corporations.

An S Corporation is not subject to federal income tax. Instead, the shareholders of the corporation are taxed on their share of the corporate income. Each shareholder pays income tax based on her personal tax rate.

Both C and S corporations incur the costs of initial registration, annual renewals and reporting. These charges can be expensive, depending on the state of incorporation.

A type of corporation commonly used by professionals in the entertainment industry like writers, producers, directors and talent is a "loanout" corporation. For this type of entity, a producer forms a corporation that she solely owns. The loanout corporation then hires, or loans out for compensation, the producer's services to a film or television studio, production company, network or any other company.

Compensation is paid to the loanout, which then pays the producer a salary or fee. The producer pays personal income taxes on such payment.

The next business structure is a limited liability company.

2. LIMITED LIABILITY COMPANY

A limited liability company is a type of business entity which is separate and distinct from its owners, called members, which can be individuals or other businesses.

Members who manage such a legal entity are called managers or managing members. The name of a limited liability company should end with either "Limited Liability Company," "LLC" or "L.L.C." to designate it as such a business entity.

This structure combines the benefits of corporations and partnerships. It protects members from responsibility for company debt. It also creates a "pass-through" of income and expenses for each member according to the membership agreement.

A partnership, below, is a different entity.

3. PARTNERSHIP

A partnership is a business entity owned by two or more persons or other business entities called "partners." Several types of partnerships exist, as described below.

The name of the partnership may end in "GP," "LP," or "LLP," with or without periods between the letters as the partners deem appropriate. In some jurisdictions, these ending initials are not required.

Types of partnerships are listed below:

- *General Partnership ("GP").* In this entity, the owners are all general partners who share equally in the management, profits and liabilities of the partnership. In such partnership, each of the partners are liable for partnership debts, rather than being protected from such liabilities.
- *Limited Partnership ("LP").* This entity requires one or more general partners to be responsible for management and debts of one or more limited partners. The limited partners in an LP make no management decisions and are not liable for company debts except as stated in the articles of partnership. Such liability is generally limited to each member's capital investment.
- *Limited Liability Partnership ("LLP").* The owners of this entity are "partners." They may be shielded from liability or not, depending on state regulations. In some states, this entity may only be formed by certain professionals like lawyers, accountants and architects, while in others anyone may form an LLP and own it.

4. SOLE PROPRIETOR/DBA/FICTITIOUS BUSINESS

A sole proprietor is simply an individual who operates a business without forming a legal business entity. The owner may operate under his own name or may file a fictitious business statement, otherwise known as a "DBA" or a "Doing Business As" statement.

A DBA is not a legal entity but merely a name which an owner uses to operate his business. An example is "Jack Smith DBA Uniquely My Film Productions."

A primary benefit of operating as a sole proprietor is the lack of many formal legal requirements. Even the fictitious name is often optional.

A fictitious business statement is the public filing of a business name under which a sole proprietor will operate. The public identifies the business by such name.

For a DBA, a producer files a fictitious business statement in the city or county where he works or operates his business activities. Most jurisdictions require that a public notice be published about the formation of the business and its owner. In many areas, it must be published in the "Legal News" section of a local newspaper before starting business operations.

A producer with a DBA who operates a sole proprietorship and receives income for producing services is subject to state and federal personal tax on the income. Business income and expenses are reported on Schedule C of the producer's personal federal income tax return.

The major drawback of a producer operating as a sole proprietorship, with or without a fictitious business name, is the producer's sole responsibility for debts. There is no shield or protection against business liabilities. Creditors can sue a sole proprietor personally for non-payment of debts and can collect on a judgment by seizing personal property like cars, real estate, bank accounts and other assets.

B. FORMING A BUSINESS ENTITY

Most state Secretary of State or business development offices are usually the entities responsible for accepting filings for new business entities in the state for corporations, limited liability companies, partnerships and others. An agent for service of process for litigation is required. The agent may be the owner, a third-party agent or a company located and operating in the state.

After forming a new business, the owner or owners must fulfill other conditions before starting to do business. They must select the parties who will manage the business.

For example, corporate shareholders select the directors. Partners in a partnership select one or more managing partners.

Immediately upon formation, the initial meeting of the owners of the company should be held. A person should be appointed, elected or hired to keep written minutes of the initial meeting including a record of all motions, votes and management decisions for the company.

Regular meetings should be held at least annually with written records like minutes of the meetings as proof of continued operations. However, some states have no requirement for annual meetings.

A minimum of formalities must be followed to shield the producer owner from liability. These may include having a separate bank account in the name of the company, sending notices of meetings, recording meeting minutes, and keeping records on decisions.

Creditors may try to "pierce the corporate veil" by suing a shareholder personally for corporate debts. They may succeed if the corporate formalities and the corporation's separate existence are not respected.

C. EIN

A new business entity must also obtain a federal Employer Identification Number ("EIN") from the Internal Revenue Service and a state tax number for quarterly and annual tax returns from the state tax authority.

States usually grant sales tax exemption certificates to businesses on material purchases for later resale or use in products to resell. The company could be exempt from paying taxes on materials bought for duplication, or on other goods for resale.

D. OTHER FILING REQUIREMENTS

Numerous other filings are also required for business entities, such as annual renewals, franchise filings and other reports necessary to maintain the entity's good standing. Depending on the entity's income and assets in the state and other criteria, these fees and costs can range from a few dollars to thousands per year.

Counties and cities may have additional requirements like operational or occupational licenses for the business. Prior to transacting any business in a location, an owner should verify all tax and license requirements.

*

In summary, producers can choose from a variety of legal business structures which they can operate. Industry professionals can also own a loanout corporation that hires out their services to third parties.

The decision as to the best business structure for a producer or creative professional is subject to each person's needs and perspectives on debt, ownership, revenues and taxation.

3.

HIRE AN ENTERTAINMENT ATTORNEY

Listen! Hear the groans at the mention of an attorney? Many producers dislike the idea of having an entertainment attorney on board the production...until the film runs into problems. Then the lawyer becomes a lifesaver, a genius, a brilliant tactician in the battle to raise film financing or handle production issues.

At that point producers are so happy they planned ahead and hired production counsel before the issues erupted. If not, they may be mired with production problems that cost much more to resolve than if the entertainment lawyer had been hired early on.

Even Shakespeare got into the game, seemingly. In *Henry VI*, Part II, Act IV, Scene II, the character Dick the Butcher states, "First thing we do, let's kill all the lawyers." But that line is highly misunderstood by the general public.

In Shakespeare's time, lawyers were considered a noble group who defended and protected the law. Rather than referring to lawyers as "bad guys" to get rid of, the meaning of Shakespeare's dialogue shows the criminals intended to do away with the ethical lawyers who could thwart their nefarious acts. This would clear the path for the rebel Jack to become the leader in the resulting chaos and lawlessness.

What types of questions should you ask an entertainment attorney before engaging his or her services? Some such queries are below, many of which can be answered by visiting the attorney's or law firm's website and studying attorney profiles, fee structure, representative clients, services offered, and so on.

If you are unable to learn the answers beforehand, set up an initial consultation with an attorney. Confirm in advance whether it is complimentary and the length of time allowed. Most entertainment attorneys will provide a short initial meeting by phone or in person at no cost to the potential client.

Consider using some or all of the questions below during the initial meeting. The process is as beneficial for the producer in interviewing the attorney as it is for the lawyer who must determine whether to accept him as a client.

1. *Are you licensed to practice law in my state?*

Finding attorneys via the internet sometimes results in finding out-of-state practitioners. While it is unethical and, in many cases, illegal, for an attorney to provide legal advice to a person or entity in a jurisdiction in which the attorney is not licensed, it does happen. This is an important requirement for any lawyer to meet before a producer should consider signing an engagement agreement or paying a retainer or other fee.

2. *What type of clients do you represent?*

Seek a lawyer who generally works with producers or production companies similar to you or yours in size and type of work.

3. *What services do you provide?*

Independent producers and small to mid-size production companies generally cannot afford in-house legal counsel or business affairs departments. It is important to hire a lawyer who can provide all the services needed for costs that fit the budget.

Hiring multiple lawyers to do multiple tasks is costly and time-consuming. Each lawyer must be brought up to speed by the producer or the other lawyer, or lawyers, on other work previously done. To do so, each lawyer incurs time and expenses for such communications. If they bill the producer by the hour, this could add up to substantial additional fees. In such a situation, it is important that services are not duplicated.

Every lawyer has a unique approach to entertainment law, even considering the general practices and standards in this field.

Hiring multiple lawyers may result in receiving different approaches to an issue. This leaves the producer in the middle, facing conflicting advice.

It is also more expedient to work with one entertainment attorney who can provide all the necessary services rather than multiple attorneys in a firm or from several firms.

4. *Do you work on a contingency fee basis?*

Legal fees and rates vary from one legal jurisdiction to another and are subject to ethical and legal requirements of the particular jurisdiction.

Rather than charging for services rendered on an hourly basis, some entertainment attorneys will work on a contingency fee basis.

Generally, but not always, the initial payment of a retainer is required. Other attorneys require initial retainers against which they bill on a monthly basis for their time and expenses.

Still other attorneys charge a combination of reduced hourly rates plus a small contingency.

5. *Are you a transactional or a trial lawyer (or both)?*

Entertainment attorneys may offer transactional services only, or transactional and mediation, arbitration and/or litigation.

Transactional lawyers focus on contract drafting and deal negotiation, rather than litigation. Some attorneys also participate in alternative dispute resolution procedures like mediation or arbitration. Entertainment trial attorneys may provide transactional work, though many focus on litigation and/or mediation and arbitration. Alternative dispute resolution methods are in Chapter 6 of this book.

6. *How do you determine your fees and costs?*

An attorney's fee schedule should be included in the engagement agreement, which is the contract signed by the lawyer and the producer or production company.

For the benefit of the parties, it is important that the attorney detail all fees and expenses in a written fee agreement signed by both parties. This will also eliminate misunderstandings, confusion and potential conflict between the producer and the attorney later in the production.

Sometimes lawyers charge a percentage of their total bill to cover expenses such as paralegals, online research, photocopies, facsimiles, postage and other such costs.

Other times, out-of-pocket costs are specified to the penny or exact expenses are billed with a profit mark-up.

If any later agreements are made to fee arrangements, these should be in writing also.

7. *Do you obtain tax credit certification and negotiate tax credit sales?*

Some entertainment attorneys work in jurisdictions that grant film production tax credits. As part of their services, some will procure the tax credit pre-certification and post-certification approvals before and after production.

It is possible they will also negotiate sales of these credits for the producers after production and post-production of a film are completed.

While certain entertainment attorneys will provide both of these services, many entertainment lawyers will provide one or the other, or neither.

Tax credit sales generate funding for the producers after the production is completed and usually after the jurisdiction conducts or approves an audit of the production expenditures. Some jurisdictions provide direct rebates to producers after such completion and audit or expenditure accounting review. Tax credits are discussed in further detail in Chapter 15 of the book.

In certain jurisdictions, third-party lenders provide loans against future tax credits to be earned. Chapter 17 provides more information on tax credit loans.

8. *Do you have experience in (choose the services and contracts in which you are interested)?*
    - Corporate/LLC/Loanout formation;

FINANCING INDEPENDENT FILMS | 35

- Option and acquisition agreements;
- Screenplay options;
- Book-to-film adaptation agreements;
- Development deals;
- Co-production agreements;
- International co-production contracts;
- Talent agreements;
- Director agreements;
- Producer agreements;
- Crew agreements;
- Composer agreements;
- Completion bond contracts;
- Multi-party financing agreements;
- Insurance contracts;
- Film sale and pre-sale agreements;
- Producer's representative services;
- Festival sales;
- Distribution agreements; and
- Any other services you need.

9. *Do you have client references of prior productions and producers you've represented in the same budget range as my film?*

This is an important question that many producers and filmmakers omit when interviewing an entertainment attorney. The lawyer must obtain permission from other clients before providing them as a reference. If that occurs, a prospective client filmmaker should research the films made by the clients before talking with them about their working relationship with the lawyer and what work he did for them.

Though producers may have numerous other questions, these are generally the most important needed to determine what type of entertainment attorney to hire and why.

For productions on a limited budget, a producer can attempt to negotiate a fixed fee with an entertainment attorney to provide all the services that are needed on the production.

Some entertainment attorneys will exclude criminal, securities, litigation and other matters, restricting a fixed fee to certain transactional services. However, the final agreement is negotiated by the producer and the attorney.

Every producer should budget a fixed amount for entertainment legal services that will set the production on the right path and keep it there. On a limited budget, producers could limit the services they need. They could negotiate with an attorney to prepare "form contracts" for the film, like agreements for talent, crew and locations. They could also hire an entertainment attorney to assist during only certain specific periods of filmmaking, such as development, production or distribution.

Also, some entertainment lawyers offer producer's representative services to help market and exploit the film, such as at festivals.

In the end, every production has legal issues. While some are greater than others, producers can resolve problems quicker or prevent costly errors by hiring an experienced entertainment lawyer early in the process.

4.

ACQUIRE LITERARY MATERIAL RIGHTS

All producers and filmmakers who are not screenwriters themselves need to know how to acquire the rights to literary material for a film. This means understanding how to obtain intellectual property rights to screenplays, books, newspaper articles, or other types of copyrighted property on which screenplays and films may be based.

These intellectual property works are the foundation of a film. A feature film cannot be made without a script. Thus, it is important to understand the process of how to obtain the rights to material to adapt for a screenplay.

A. ACQUIRING ORIGINAL SCREENPLAYS

Before a producer or filmmaker acquires the rights to literary material, it is important to determine the type of material sought and the purpose. Subsequently, an agreement to acquire the rights can be negotiated.

The two types of original screenplays that producers generally seek to acquire are:
1. A "Spec" script which exists and was previously written by a screenwriter on the "speculation" of a sale; and
2. A "Work-for-hire" script to be written once a screenwriter is hired by and under the direction of an employer. A studio, production company or independent producer can hire the writer to write a screenplay according to the employer's instructions.

Two types of agreements commonly used to obtain rights to a screenplay are:
1. Option and acquisition agreements; and
2. Work-for-hire agreements.

Each of these agreements grants a producer certain rights regarding a screenplay. However, unlike option and acquisition agreements and work-for-hire agreements, a script option does not grant ownership rights until it is bought.

For both an option and acquisition agreement and a work-for-hire agreement, an assignment agreement is used to transfer the rights at the time of the purchase. These rights, including copyright, are transferred from the screenwriter or other owner to the producer or producing entity when the script is acquired.

The assignment is a sale and transfer of these rights. Upon signing the agreement, the screenwriter seller transfers ownership of the rights to the producer buyer. The agreement defines whether some or all of the rights are sold and if the writer retains any rights.

The discussion that follows discusses the typical agreements used to acquire rights to literary materials, including, but not limited to, screenplays.

1. OPTION AND ACQUISITION

An option and acquisition agreement is a contract to purchase certain rights to a literary property.

An option is an exclusive license granted by an "Optionor" screenwriter or other owner of a previously-written screenplay to an "Optionee" producer or other party. The option grants the optionee a limited period of time to decide whether to buy the screenplay rights described in the option at the end of the term from the optionor.

The option term is typically limited to a specific period, which may be months or years. The agreement may include one or more option extensions, usually at an additional fee. The purchase price should be stated in the contract so that the optionor and the optionee understand the costs as well as all of the conditions required.

While the purchase price is usually stated as a fixed-dollar price, it could be specified as a percentage of the budget of the film anticipated to be produced.

40 | ACQUIRE LITERARY MATERIAL RIGHTS

The timing of payment of the acquisition price may vary. The optionor might require full payment at the exercise of the option. Or, he might be willing to wait until the first day of principal photography. Then again, he could require a partial payment at the exercise of the option and the balance paid within a certain period, or on the first day of principal photography of the film.

In an option and acquisition agreement, the writer who owns the exclusive rights of copyright in his screenplay negotiates a deal with the optionee, who is a potential buyer, to acquire one or more of the rights.

Producers or studios may contract with screenwriters to write or re-write original screenplays or to adapt literary material they own, such as books or life stories. They often choose to negotiate option and acquisition agreements with writers for existing "spec" screenplays, and then develop them with other writers and directors.

The option part of the agreement is an exclusive license. This allows a potential buyer, the optionee, to pay a nominal sum to "lock up" the rights to a screenplay for a limited term to fulfill conditions she needs prior to buying the rights. These might include raising financing, attaching a director or lead actor or getting a distribution deal.

If the producer is unable to fulfill her conditions or changes her mind, she simply lets the option expire. The producer loses her option money and moves on. The writer is then free to sell the script to someone else.

The acquisition part of the agreement is the sale of the rights by the writer or owner to the optionee. At this point, the optionee exercises the option and pays the purchase price. When the exercise occurs, the copyright owner sells, transfers and assigns the ownership of the rights to the optionee buyer.

Since optionees often need additional time to exercise the option, this agreement generally grants the optionee a right of renewal. To effect a renewal, the optionee merely pays additional option fees to the owner just prior to the expiration of the original term.

Such extension is automatically exercised by the optionee's payment to the owner. This gives the producer more time to raise her financing and accomplish other tasks prior to exercising the option.

If no option extension exists, or if the original option term ends without a right of renewal, the producer must decide whether to exercise the option and purchase the rights, re-negotiate a renewal, or walk away and lose any option fees paid.

If the producer exercises the option, she buys the screenplay, pays the screenwriter per the previously-agreed terms and proceeds with her production.

If the option is not exercised, the producer's right to acquire the script terminates and all the rights granted in the option return to the screenplay owner.

This is referred to as the "reversionary right" or "turnaround" since the rights literally turn around from optionee and revert back to optionor. If this occurs, the screenwriter controls the rights again and can option or sell the screenplay to someone else.

In the option agreement, a common term during reversion requires the subsequent optionee of the screenplay to repay the original optionee's development costs. The screenwriter must include these costs as a term of any subsequent option or sale agreements.

The screenwriter should not be held responsible for such development costs, but the next optionee would be required to repay the earlier optionee upon exercise of the option and purchase of the screenplay.

The option and acquisition agreement is a valuable tool for a writer to license rights to his property on fixed purchase terms. But as an alternative to an option and acquisition agreement, some producers and production companies enter into work-for-hire agreements with writers, as follows.

2. WORK-FOR-HIRE

A motion picture production company may commission a screenwriter on a work-for-hire agreement to write an original or adapted screenplay, or to rewrite an existing script. Or the production company may hire the writer on an employment agreement for such work. In both instances, the writer's services are considered a "work-for-hire" per the contract or employment agreement.

U.S. copyright law defines a "work-for-hire," also called a "work-made-for-hire," as a work that falls into one of two categories:
- A work that is prepared by an employee within the scope of his employment; or
- A work that is specially ordered or commissioned for use as part of a motion picture or other audiovisual work or dramatic work, including a screenplay.

In this instance, the writer creates the work but the production company is the copyright author and owner according to law. The writer does not own any copyright in the screenplay or the rewrites that he completes under the work-for-hire contract.

Each person who provides services to a film should sign a work-for-hire agreement, including screenwriters, producers, talent, directors, editors, music composers, set designers, art directors, and other crew and creatives involved in the film.

Producers should always use work-for-hire agreements to assure they have complete ownership of the entire copyright in a film. Otherwise, the people rendering creative services to a film would own the copyright in the results and proceeds of their work, rather than the producer or production company.

A discussion follows on the acquisition of the rights to adapt a book into a film.

B. ACQUIRING BOOK-TO-FILM ADAPTATION RIGHTS

When a producer or director wants to adapt a book into a screenplay for a feature film, a contract is necessary to obtain the rights for such adaptation. Since the book is the original work, the screenplay based on the book becomes the derivative work. See Chapter 5 for more detailed information on copyrights and derivative works.

The process is the same to acquire the rights to adapt books or other original literary materials, such as newspaper articles and short stories, into a screenplay and a feature film. The contract that is typically used to acquire adaptation rights is an option and acquisition, as described above in Part A for screenplay acquisitions.

Similar to acquiring a screenplay, a book adaptation option and acquisition agreement is an exclusive option. For a nominal fee, the owner of the book rights grants a producer a fixed period to decide whether to buy them.

During the option period, the producer determines if she will buy the rights and move ahead to produce a film. The producer may write the adapted screenplay herself. Or she might invest in development costs by hiring one or more screenwriters on a work-for-hire basis to adapt the book into a screenplay.

The producer or production company that hires the writer or writers is the owner of the copyright in the finished screenplay and all drafts, rewrites and polishes. But the screenplay may not be produced unless the owner sells and transfers the adaptation rights.

Once the book-to-film adaptation rights are purchased, the buyer producer or production company owns the legal rights to produce the film from the adapted screenplay.

The legal rights that are purchased are transferred from the seller to the buyer through a legal document known as an assignment, discussed in the next section.

C. ASSIGNMENTS

When a producer acquires all the rights, including copyright, from the owner of a screenplay or a book for adaptation to a film, the parties execute an assignment agreement. This is a standard contract used to transfer all the exclusive rights (which may or may not include the French "droit moral" or "moral rights") from the copyright owner to the buyer.

This contract assigns, or transfers, the rights being acquired from the owner to the producer. Once the acquisition agreement and the assignment have been fully executed, the owner no longer has any claim to the ownership of the rights that were assigned. And the owner no longer has the right to use the rights. The buyer who acquires the rights from the owner is the sole and exclusive owner of the rights that were transferred.

An assignment may be a short form or a long form agreement. While some are found on the internet, it is always recommended that producers consult legal counsel for specific agreements relating to a specific film or contractual agreement before signing it.

Sometimes a producer or director may wish to write a screenplay based on an original work which is copyrighted by the owner of that work. Such works include books, poetry, short stories, newspaper articles, and the like.

The subject of copyright ownership of intellectual property rights in original screenplays as well as in work-for-hire scripts is discussed in Chapter 5, which follows.

5.

COPYRIGHT YOUR WORK

Copyright is an exclusive legal right granted by law to creators of original, creative works of authorship that are fixed in a tangible medium of expression. Issued in 1777, Article I, Section 8 of the U.S. Constitution embodies the "Copyright Clause," the cornerstone of copyright law stating, "The Congress shall have Power...To promote the Progress of Science and useful Arts, by securing for limited Times to Authors and Inventors the exclusive Right to their respective Writings and Discoveries."

This Chapter gives copyright requirements for a film and its underlying screenplay, with examples of what is and is not copyrightable.

A. IDEAS ARE NOT COPYRIGHTABLE

Ideas are not copyrightable. Only the expression of an idea that is fixed in a tangible medium of expression can be protected by copyright. These concepts are discussed later in this Chapter. Even so, if this idea is the only way for someone to convey that concept, such as a mathematical formula or the boy meets girl/boy loses girl/boy gets girl romantic comedy scenario, it cannot be copyrighted.

Copyright is secured in a screenplay when it is creative and in a fixed form. Each rewrite and polish that is printed, written, saved to a computer or flash drive or otherwise fixed in a tangible medium of expression is a new derivative work of the original copyrightable screenplay. Requirements are discussed below.

B. REQUIREMENTS

To be eligible for copyright protection, a work must meet the two criteria below:
- The work must be an original work of authorship which includes at least some creative effort; and
- The work must be fixed in a tangible medium of expression.

1. CREATIVITY

To meet the creativity requirement, the author must create a copyrightable work of authorship which is original and creative.

The added requirement of creative effort was not in the Constitution. Creativity was determined later, in 1991, by the U.S. Supreme Court to be a necessity for a copyrightable work. The case was *Feist*

Publications vs. Rural Telephone Service Co., 499 U.S. 340 (1991). In this case, the Court held that a white pages telephone directory of an alphabetical listing of names, addresses and numbers did not qualify for copyright because it lacked a minimum of creative effort.

Since the *Feist* case, creativity is an important prerequisite for copyrighting works. An original work must embody at least some creativity to be copyrighted. The law does not specify how much "creative effort" is required but merely copying names and addresses is not sufficient.

2. FIXED IN A TANGIBLE MEDIUM

The second requirement for copyright is that the work be "fixed in a tangible medium of expression." This means putting the work into a physical form, a concrete medium, or another means to perceive the expression of an idea.

The work may be fixed directly if it is able to be seen or heard after it is first spoken, performed, filmed or otherwise fixed. Examples of direct fixation of a work include writing changes on a printed script or noting script revisions on a legal pad.

Otherwise, the work may be fixed indirectly. This is done with the assistance of a device or machine, like recording notes for a script or saving a rewrite onto a disk.

Thinking about or mentioning a story idea, screenplay revision or film scene change is still just an idea that cannot be copyrighted. But typing the change into a device, saving work on a drive, or writing it by hand fixes the expression of an idea in a tangible medium able to be perceived directly or indirectly.

Expressing a story idea for a feature film to your friend in an elevator is not fixed in a tangible medium. That is only a spoken idea that could be overheard and used by anyone without any liability. You just shared your idea orally, but that idea was not expressed in a tangible medium to be perceived later. And although it is not a good idea to talk about ideas in a crowded elevator, recording the conversation would turn the idea into an expression fixed in a tangible medium.

Similarly, suppose a writer discusses possible screenplay changes with a studio or production company executive but does not document them. The changes are ideas but not copyrightable unless written, typed, saved, recorded or otherwise fixed. Then the changes can be perceived directly or indirectly by a device and are copyrightable.

C. DERIVATIVE WORKS

If you copy or use part of a third party's copyrighted work with the owner's authorization, the new work you create is not "original." It is a "derivative work" derived from and based on a prior creative work. A screenplay adapted from a newspaper or magazine article, book or other source is considered a derivative work.

Using a derivative work requires written authorization from the original work's owner. This authorization can be granted in the option and acquisition agreement in which the studio, screenwriter, production company, producer or director acquires the rights to write a screenplay based on the original source.

If you attempt to create a derivative work of a copyrighted work without authorization, your work infringes on the owner's copyright. This could subject you to a lawsuit for damages and possible criminal proceedings unless you have a defense, such as fair use.

Fair use defenses include news reporting, education, scholarship, research, commentary or critique and parody. Feature film derivative works generally cannot use the fair use defense except in rare occasions such as parody. When copyright exists in a work is discussed below.

D. WHEN COPYRIGHT EXISTS

At the moment that an original work of authorship is created and fixed in a tangible medium of expression, copyright exists and is secured in the work, even without registration with the U.S. Copyright Office ("USCO").

Registration is a formal legal filing with the USCO required by U.S. copyright law. Filing creates a public record of the facts of a copyrighted work, such as the owner, title, type of work and more. The process is simple, inexpensive, and does not require an attorney. The USCO offers paper copyright forms but encourages less-costly, faster-processed filings electronically on www.copyright.gov.

Works may be copyrighted by a single author using his own name or a pseudonym or registered anonymously. Multiple authors may register a work as co-authors or joint authors.

Registration with the USCO of a work that is copyrightable is highly recommended for the many benefits it provides, especially statutory damages and legal fees in an infringement case.

For more on copyrights, see the Contact page or order other Copyright Handbooks by this author wherever books are sold:

- ©*HEAP PROTECTION: COPYRIGHT HANDBOOK FOR FILMS;*
- ©*HEAP PROTECTION: COPYRIGHT HANDBOOK FOR SCREENPLAYS;*
- ©*HEAP PROTECTION: COPYRIGHT HANDBOOK FOR TELEPLAYS;*
- ©*HEAP PROTECTION: COPYRIGHT HANDBOOK FOR TV PROJECTS;*
- *CHEAP ℗ROTECTION: COPYRIGHT HANDBOOK FOR MUSIC;* and,
- ©*HEAP PROTECTION: COPYRIGHT HANDBOOK FOR LITERARY WORKS.*

6.

USE ALTERNATIVE DISPUTE RESOLUTION

When an unauthorized party uses a copyrighted work, he infringes on the work. Instead of taking the infringer to court, a copyright owner can elect one or more Alternative Dispute Resolution ("ADR") methods to settle the conflict.

ADR procedures are mediation, arbitration and med-arb, a combination of mediation and arbitration. Another type of ADR is World Intellectual Property Organization ("WIPO") international dispute resolution.

Mediation is the first method discussed.

A. MEDIATION

In mediation, a neutral third party assists the disputing parties to resolve differences. The neutral is often an ADR-trained lawyer or retired judge, whose fees and expenses are split between the parties.

The parties do not need to be represented by lawyers in mediation. However, in disputes with large damage claims, attorneys and forensic accountants can present legal and financial analysis for their respective parties.

Typically, each party makes a statement of his case in one room. The parties then separate into different rooms. The mediator meets with each party individually to assess the value, strengths and weaknesses of his claim. He assists the parties but does not decide the case.

To reach a resolution, the copyright owner may reduce his damage claim, license his work or forego other demands. The infringer may agree to pay to license or purchase the work.

If a settlement is reached, the parties sign a binding contract for their obligations to each other. A party may sue the other party if he fails to comply with the final agreement.

Mediation is voluntary unless required by a contract with a mediation clause. The process is an efficient, low-cost way to settle disputes and resolve conflicts without litigation or other legal remedies.

B. ARBITRATION

Arbitration is an ADR proceeding similar to a trial, though more informal. The parties may choose a neutral organization to supervise the arbitration. Rules regarding discovery, experts, evidence, witness testimony and other issues are set forth and implemented by the supervisory organization.

The disputing parties mutually agree on one or more neutral parties as arbitrators to supervise the arbitration and to issue a final determination and an arbitral award. A party may represent himself or choose to be represented by an attorney.

Many organizations require arbitration to be final and binding so the proceeding can fully and completely resolve all issues.

For claims under about $100,000, ADR organizations offer expedited, streamlined arbitration, less costly than larger cases.

1. Guild Arbitration

Writers and production companies in the entertainment industry that are signatories to entertainment Guild collective bargaining agreements are subject to the arbitration clauses in those agreements.

Several Guilds whose agreements have arbitration clauses include the Directors Guild of America ("DGA"), SAG/AFTRA and the Writers Guild of America ("WGA"). Non-signatories to these agreements do not implement Guild rules, but they may use other organizations for arbitration.

The Appendix in the back of the book provides contact information for certain Guilds, unions and ADR providers.

2. Private ADR Providers

Entertainment industry professionals and companies not bound to Guild or union ADR clauses often choose a private organization that can administer mediation, binding arbitration, discovery, neutral expert analysis, mini-trials and more.

To proceed with any mediation or arbitration, the parties in the dispute must select the mediator or arbitrator. They must also agree to the proceeding, the rules of the organization and the forum, or location, where the proceeding is to take place.

For arbitrations, the parties must also agree whether the decision reached by the arbitrator or arbitrator panel will be final and binding. If so, suit may be filed to enforce the decision if breached by a party. If not, the parties may choose other methods to resolve the disputed agreement.

Three major private ADR providers are:
- IFTA®: Independent Film & Television Alliance®;
- JAMS®; and
- American Arbitration Association®.

Each of these three alternative dispute resolution providers are described in the summary that follows.

IFTA® Arbitration is provided by the Independent Film & Television Alliance®, a global non-profit trade association of distributors and producers of independent film and television productions. It offers mediation and arbitration services with

IFTA® rules for IFTA® members and non-members relating to disputes relating to production, finance and distribution. The association's website is www.ifta-online.org.

JAMS® is an organization offering ADR administration procedures for disputes around the world in many fields, including entertainment and Intellectual Property. The website is www.jamsadr.com.

The American Arbitration Association® is an ADR organization with offices within and outside the United States that offers dispute resolution administration for IP, entertainment, and many other types of cases. The website is www.adr.org.

C. MED/ARB

The combination of both mediation and arbitration called "Med/Arb" is a form of ADR. It is often used by entertainment professionals and other companies to resolve disputes. Using this method, the parties first attempt to mediate with a jointly-chosen neutral who attempts to navigate them toward a solution.

If the mediation process is unsuccessful, the parties then commence arbitration, using a different neutral as the arbitrator.

D. WIPO DISPUTE RESOLUTION

WIPO, the World Intellectual Property Organization, offers a neutral forum to resolve disputes outside court in three ways:

1. Mediation: In this process, an impartial third party directs a mutually-agreeable resolution between parties in the process.

2. Arbitration: In this procedure, an impartial third party reviews the dispute and issues a decision and award to settle the conflict. The parties decide in advance if the decision will be final and binding to resolve the case, or if they will reserve rights to other resolution methods, including litigation.

3. Expert Determination: When the parties disagree on an issue in a dispute, they may agree to hire one or more WIPO experts to determine answers to specific issues, including copyright value or technical questions.

F. COPYRIGHT CLAIMS BOARD

NEW! In December 2020, the Copyright Alternative Small-Claims Enforcement Act ("CASE") was enacted which established a Copyright Claims board in the USCO office for dispute resolution. Visit the USCO website, www.copyright.gov, for more information.

*

A crucial decision a producer must make is how to market the film and whether to engage a film marketing expert early in the process, or at all. Such film marketing professionals are discussed in the next Chapter.

7.

HIRE FILM MARKETING PROFESSIONALS

Before a producer starts raising funds for a budget to begin development, she should decide on the potential markets for the film and how she plans to sell it.

Five types of industry professionals serve as middlemen who assist film producers in marketing their films to domestic distributors, end buyers and foreign buyers in international markets. The lower the budget and the less-known the cast and director, the more difficult this job is. These five categories are:
- Producer's Reps (Representatives);
- Executive Producers, or "EPs";
- Foreign Sales Agents;
- Television Sales Agents; and
- Aggregators.

Some industry professionals also include a category for a producer of marketing and development. However, these functions can be provided by someone in the other categories or they can be allocated to one person on the production team experienced in these tasks.

Does a producer really need any of these professionals? Obviously, they add costs to the bottom line. Some filmmakers do not hire middlemen because of the fees and costs involved. These may be upfront, contingent on a sale, or a combination. Others need but do not understand the value of a middleman, which may not be the same for every film.

Each of these categories is described in the pages that follow. The first is a Producer's Rep.

1. PRODUCER'S REP

A Producer's Representative, often called a Producer's Rep, is an industry middleman who works on the producer's behalf to sell a film to one or more theatrical distributors in the North American market (the U.S. and Canada). For television sales, a producer should consider a TV Sales Agent or Aggregator, discussed later. Producers are often able to sell their film into home video themselves, without a Producer's Rep.

The success of a Producer's Rep's efforts depends largely on the film quality, cast and director, as well as the filmmaker's prior film experience and success. A Producer's Rep should have strong relationships with domestic distributors. But a film that generates buzz or is accepted into a major film festival often captures the attention of theatrical distributors without such a Rep.

FINANCING INDEPENDENT FILMS | 61

Not all Producer's Rep contracts are alike. They vary with Producer's Reps themselves. Sometimes the Producer's Rep licenses the film directly from the producer and pays for all domestic rights but keeps all sales revenues. Other Producer's Reps charge an upfront fee or a fee plus a percentage of all sales, regardless of whether the Rep or the producer sold the film to the buyers. Still other Producer's Reps may agree to be paid if and when the film sells.

Producer's Reps offer different contracts for different films. The important thing to do is negotiate, negotiate, negotiate. If a Producer's Rep asks for an upfront fee, try to lower or eliminate it.

An upfront fee usually means the Rep is not very confident in his ability to sell the film and cover his costs, so the fee covers that risk. However, a film with a great story and cast (even if unknown) may justify a Producer's Rep charging a contingency fee based on a percentage of sales.

What percentage does a Producer's Rep charge? It varies and can range from 5% to 15%. The lower rate is rare and is usually reserved for good pre-existing relationships between the Rep and the producer or the talent. A Rep may reduce his fee for films with an acclaimed or award-winning cast or director.

A producer should always review the contract prior to engaging a Producer's Rep.

If the producer is represented by an entertainment lawyer as discussed in Chapter 3, the lawyer will review all contracts carefully and explain them to the producer. Important terms include the specific fees and expenses due by the producer during the contract and after its termination, responsibilities undertaken by the Producer's Rep, and penalties in the event of a breach.

For example, suppose a Producer's Rep attends a film market, offers your film in his catalogue along with his twenty other films but no one buys yours. Then you attend the same film market a year later and sell your film. Do you owe the Producer's Rep a fee for the sale?

It depends on the contract terms, like whether the Producer's Rep actually pitched the film to the eventual buyer. Pitching in this case could be something as simple as emailing the catalogue or a list of films for sale, including yours, to the potential buyer.

Depending on the contract, a fee may still be due if anyone who received the Rep's email buys the film within a certain period of time. This is only one reason why it is important to negotiate and understand the terms of a Rep's contract before signing it.

While a Producer's Rep might offer to sell your film internationally, producers may be better served by an experienced foreign sales company representing them. A

Producer's Rep without strong foreign distributor relationships may sub-contract with a third-party foreign sales company for international sales. Paying fees to two agent middlemen may be justified if they increase the producer's revenue stream. Sub-paragraphs 3 and 4 below give more details on Foreign and Television Sales Agents.

Producers should research other films which potential Producer's Reps have repped and sold. Then the producer should interview the Reps. Not all information may be publicly available, and some information may not be current. In any case, some of the questions to ask a Producer's Rep include:

- What film genre is your specialty?
- What films like mine have you sold?
- Which U.S. markets and festivals will you attend in the next 12 months?
- What kind of films are you seeking?
- How many films will you take this year to film markets?
- How many other films are you currently representing?
- Do you handle each film yourself, or assign them to associates?
- What are your fees, on what are they based and how are they charged?
- Do you charge any expenses, and how are they paid and recouped?
- Will you work on a contingency commission?
- Will you forego the upfront fee?

- What distributor relationships do you have?
- What services (advertising, festival strategy, marketing) do you provide?
- May I see your past catalogues?
- Have you been successful at getting films into film festivals?
- Have you gotten a theatrical (or other) release or deal for a film without screening it at a major film festival?
- How can you help me generate buzz and line up distributors for my premiere at (name) film festival?
- How do you sell a film that doesn't screen at a festival or market?
- What materials do you need from me to sell my film?
- What materials will you provide?

The next type of marketing professional is the Executive Producer who becomes part of the production team to develop and market the film.

2. EXECUTIVE PRODUCER

An Executive Producer, or "EP," often joins the producer's unit if he brings funding to the film. This may be his personal money or funds from others. In addition to raising funds, the EP wears many hats and provides very important functions for a film, including one or more of the following:

- Development with creatives;
- Creating the marketing plan to exploit the film;
- Review and oversight of copyrights, royalties, and legal contracts subject to production counsel;
- Assistance in budget creation;
- Production budget oversight to bring film in on time and on budget;
- Approving, and procuring funds for, extraordinary costs;
- On set responsibilities, if needed by the film's producers;
- Liaison with distributors, sales agents, etc. to sell the film; and
- Any other functions not handled by the producers.

Another type of marketing professional that assists the producer in selling the film is a Foreign Sales Agent. The main functions of this film marketing professional are discussed below.

3. FOREIGN SALES AGENT

A Foreign Sales Agent ("FSA"), sometimes referred to as an International Sales Agent, a Film Sales Agent or simply a Sales Agent, is a middleman that sells producers' films into international territories. For a U.S. film, these are all the territories located outside the U.S. and Canada.

FSA's represent filmmakers in licensing the right to sell their films to a distribution company for a particular international territory at a certain price. The distributor then sells the film to a buyer in the territory at a profit.

An FSA at an international film market might license the right to sell a film to a buyer in France, one in the United Kingdom and another in Japan, as well as to buyers in other international territories. The FSA makes the sales, handles the contracts, collects the revenues and then pays the producer less the FSA's commission fees and costs.

The FSA tries to license as many international territories as possible once the film is completed. The agent wants to generate as much revenue as possible from a film early in its life. A film with great buzz or a festival win helps the FSA generate greater momentum for foreign sales.

An FSA may offer to sell the film into both foreign and domestic markets, thus also acting as a Producer's Rep, for added fees and costs. Before agreeing to hire an FSA, a producer should consider the pros and cons of having one middleman handle all of these markets.

A producer may compare different distributors and find it more advantageous to keep some functions separate by using two different middlemen, despite the fees.

Or, a producer might decide to hire an FSA for international territories only and not hire a Producer's Rep. As with a Producer's Rep, a filmmaker should research potential FSA's and conduct interviews, modifying the questions in subparagraph 1 above for services, fees and costs.

The sales agent who sells films into the domestic television market is known as a Television Sales Agent.

4. TELEVISION SALES AGENT

Instead of selling into international markets, some sales agents specialize in selling films to the television markets like basic cable or premium/pay cable Pay-Per-View or Video-On-Demand ("VOD"). These agents are called Television ("TV") Sales Agents.

If a producer wishes to hire a TV Sales Agent, it is important to understand the relationships that the Agent has. Many television buyers prefer to buy multiple films for their particular audience from one seller, rather than from multiple agents.

In this market, TV Sales Agents often have the edge over other middlemen due to their large catalog of films from which to choose. And they have buyer relationships built over the years on understanding and offering the types of films the buyers want.

However, if a film has name talent, a great writer or a renowned director, a TV Sales Agent may not be necessary. A producer can contact acquisitions executives at networks by herself and pitch her film to the buyers or have her agent or attorney assist her to do so.

The fifth category of middlemen who sell films for a producer is the Aggregator.

5. AGGREGATOR

An Aggregator is a film industry middleman who obtains film digital rights for mobile devices and the internet from the producer for digital platform Video-On-Demand ("VOD") sales.

Many Aggregators work directly with a producer. They bypass other middlemen and eliminate third-party agent fees and commissions paid by the producer.

Major online vendors generally only accept films from approved Aggregators. But some smaller digital retailers accept films directly from producers.

A producer should consider selling VOD rights herself to these smaller outlets to maximize her film revenues. At the same time, hiring an Aggregator for the larger buyers and markets may make sense to a producer to maximize the value of her film.

III

GETTING THE BUDGET

Count 'em, 50 Ways

8.

THE 50 WAYS

In this book, you will actually learn 50 Ways, methods and tools to fund or reduce your budget. Everyone knows that only two ways exist to make a film based on a budget -- procure all the financing for the budget or reduce the budget, hopefully, without sacrificing story and quality. Part III provides 50 Ways to accomplish these objectives.

The methods used to finance independent films vary widely with different types of producers and filmmakers. Loans, grants, donations, tax credits, pre-sales and other ways are commonly used in film financing.

However, offering or selling ownership equity in a film is a security subject to federal securities laws, U.S. Securities and Exchange Commission ("SEC") regulations and state "blue sky" securities legislation. Such film equity securities require registration or an exemption by the SEC.

Chapter 18 explains several securities exemptions such as the new Regulation Crowdfunding process with new SEC rules, the "California Exemption" from registration for production companies in California, and other private offerings. An experienced securities attorney should be consulted before offering or selling ownership interests in a film or production company.

For more information on SEC registration exemptions for film ownership equity interests consider acquiring a new book on this subject. The author of this book has also written *FILM EQUITY CROWDFUNDING: 10 LEGAL WAYS TO SELL EQUITY IN YOUR FILM,* Volume 2 of the author's *Film Financing Series.* Contact information is found in the back of this book.

Forty-six of the 50 Ways do not involve securities and can be utilized by producers in any combination. Without selling film equity, filmmakers retain 100% ownership as they raise financing or lower the budget. The 50 Ways are divided into the following categories:

- WAYS 1-7: Skin in the Game
- WAYS 8-15: Donations & Grants
- WAYS 16-22: Products & Services
- WAYS 23-28: Team Effort
- WAYS 29-30: Locations
- WAYS 31-34: Soft Money 1: Rebates & Incentives
- WAYS 35-36: Soft Money 2: Tax Credits
- WAYS 37-38: Pre-Sales
- WAYS 39-46: Debt

- WAYS 47-50: Equity Securities

*

This book suggests that producers and filmmakers should carefully consider all of the 50 Ways before implementing one or more of them. The author did not write this book to make decisions for a producer about which of the 50 Ways to utilize. Nor did the writer stipulate which Ways are better than any of the others. Instead, the purpose of the book is to give the producer many funding alternatives.

The 50 Ways give producers the freedom to choose one or more of the Ways to implement. Before doing so, they should consider the amount of acceptable risk and consequences if the film is financed but is not profitable.

The amount of risk a producer is willing to take is a crucial decision to make before embarking on raising film financing. How will the loss of any of the producer's personal assets affect her? What will happen if the film does not sell? What can the producer do if the film generates revenues that are insufficient to repay those who believed enough in her to lend funds or invest in the film?

The topic of risk is integrated into the descriptions of the 50 Ways in the coming Chapters.

A discussion on the first seven of the 50 Ways follows.

9.

SKIN IN THE GAME
Ways 1-7 of 50 Ways

This Chapter gives the first seven of the 50 Ways to raise financing to fund or reduce your budget and produce your film.

These Ways require a producer to put her "skin in the game," meaning, to invest her personal money into her film. Each Way comes with its own advantages and disadvantages. The first consideration is that to create strong motivation for financiers and donors to fund your movie, the producer must invest her own money first.

A number of producers may be capable of accessing many of these Ways to put skin in the game. Others may not have the financial capability to do more than one.

But no matter which Way or Ways you choose, it is crucial that you invest your personal money into your own film. This proves your commitment and passion for your own project. How successful you are at raising film financing from third parties may depend on whether, and how much, you invest at the start.

If you don't have much cash in checking or savings accounts or a high credit limit on your credit cards, consider assets you own that you can sell or pledge as collateral for cash. These might include a car without a lien, a condo or home with equity for a second mortgage or equity line of credit, stocks or bonds, raw land that could be sold, leased or mortgaged, insurance with cash value, or a retirement fund.

Your personal investment should be deposited into a production bank account, separate and apart from your own accounts.

From the day a production bank account is opened, the producer should set up the production books of account. Entertainment accounting software is very useful to track money in (producer investment, donations, loans and any revenues) and money out (production costs and production company business expenses directly related to the film).

Funds in the production account must not be used for personal expenses like rent, car payments or even food. However, a production company can pay for justifiable business expenses like cell phones, internet service, and printing and copying costs of the loan package.

Rent for office space in your residence may also qualify as a business expense. Detailed records and receipts should be kept relating to the office's size as a percentage of total space in your home or apartment, usage, utilities cost and other such issues.

Before investing your money, determine the importance of making the film versus the risks involved if the film is not profitable. It may not be practical or desirable to sell a car, obtain a second mortgage or borrow against an insurance policy without asking key questions:

- Will you or your family be negatively impacted if you are unable to repay your loans or mortgages?
- Could you afford to lose assets pledged as collateral if you do not repay the loans?
- If film revenues and pledged assets do not cover the loans, could other assets be used or sold to repay the balance owed?

On the flip side, decide how passionate you are about your movie and how determined you are to do whatever it takes to access opportunities to make your budget.

Try an exercise in risk-reward evaluation. First, estimate the monetary reward you anticipate receiving from the film if it is sold.

Next, determine the amount you are at risk if the film does not succeed at the box office.

After that, decide the minimum skin in the game you believe will move the project ahead.

Then, you should be able to compare the risk and the reward before deciding how much of your own money you will invest.

More details to consider about risk are discussed next.

A. RISK

Experienced producers who have raised financing for one or more film projects understand the substantial risk involved in movie production. But filmmakers who have never raised funds to produce a film should carefully weigh the risks of the potential rewards and losses of a film.

Risk factors in film production are numerous. It might be difficult, or impossible, to raise all the funds needed to produce the film, even after using more than one or more of the 50 Ways described in this book.

For example, the film might not attract a distributor. Or the film might be distributed but not generate enough to repay the financiers. Otherwise, the lenders might get repaid from the money generated but there may be no revenues left for the producer who has invested her hard-earned funds in her film.

There are so many reasons why financing should not be raised for a film. Yet thousands of producers around the world embark on this risky venture in hopes of making their mark in the industry and their fortune along the way.

Despite the potential for monetary loss, many lenders and financiers undertake what they consider to be a "calculated risk" based on many factors. Quite often, a crucial factor is whether the producer believes in her own project strongly enough to invest personal funds before asking others to do so.

Producers always believe their films will achieve box office success. Yet the reality is that very few independent films do. Fewer still are distributed via theatrical release or sold otherwise and generate profits. Of the lucky ones with distribution deals, not all make enough to recoup the film cost.

Filmmakers with financial responsibilities, such as a family, student loans, mortgage, car note and the like, must determine whether they can afford to lose their entire monetary investment.

As a producer, consider what would happen if you lost everything you invested in your movie. If you can live with that choice, then this might be the right business for you. On the other hand, if you or your family or others would suffer because of your loss, you may wish to reconsider your decision to make films.

Losing money on a first film, or any film, should not be the end of a producer's career. Even if her film loses money, a producer who communicates with and respects investors, donors and equity owners may still be able to obtain financing for the next film.

The success of subsequent fundraising depends in part on how the producer worked with prior financiers. Of course, the story, talent, director, genre and other relevant specifics of the subsequent production are also important. People who donate to or invest in a film also appreciate regular communications and expect invitations to exciting perks like set visits, premieres, or being an extra in the film.

Chapter 18 provides more information on selling equity securities in a film and securities registration exemptions.

B. WAYS 1 - 7 OF 50

If you are still prepared to invest your own money, read the rest of this Chapter. If you are not prepared to put your own skin in the game, you should still read this Chapter before continuing to the other Ways in this book. Understand that many, if not most, investors will not contribute funding unless the producer puts the first money into her film.

The first Way to raise money is by investing personal cash as skin in the game.

Way 1: Your Cash

One of the first questions potential financiers ask producers before they even consider participating in financing a film is "how much skin in the game do you have?"

Financiers want to know that you, the producer, believe in your own film enough to invest your own cash into the project. Their logic is reasonable. If you as the force behind the movie do not believe in your project enough to risk your own money, why should anyone else, particularly them?

But by investing your own funds in your movie, you complete three very critical steps from the viewpoint of a film financier:
1. Prove your strong belief in your project;
2. Risk your personal funds;
3. Create built-in equity and lower risk for financiers.

Way 2 is using personal credit cards as a source of film financing. This Way is discussed in the following section.

Way 2: Your Credit Card(s)

Whoa, you say. I don't have a dollar to spare. I'm scraping by. I can barely pay my rent and car note. The entire reason why I need a financier to give me money for my film is so that I can receive a salary, pay my rent, pay my car note, pay me to live the lifestyle to which I could become accustomed, et cetera.

To those of you who think this way, I can only advise that you be positive, not negative. See the glass (the film budget) as half-full, not half-empty. Visualize your goal of a completed film and don't let anything stand in your way (legally). Direct your passion in a focused way to make film financing your priority.

A financier never wants to hear about how much money you need (especially for rent or personal expenses), but rather, two things:
1. That he or she is not the first one to invest in the movie (you are); and

FINANCING INDEPENDENT FILMS | 81

2. That your focus is to repay him or her from film revenues following a well-planned strategy.

The third Way to raise financing for a film is through marketable securities, as follows.

Way 3: Your Stocks & Bonds

Way 3 is an easy Way to get film funding. If you have investments in marketable securities like stocks and bonds, they can be sold easily to yield quick cash for you.

Are you the type of person who prefers to hold on to your securities waiting for more and more profit? If so, take a tip from wealthy investors. They pre-determine a generous rate of return, such as on a specific stock. Then they set an automatic trigger or alert for that price.

When the asset reaches that point, the person sells it to reap the profit and re-invest or use the funds for another purpose. Thus, even if the stock prices increase beyond that point, the investors don't feel they have lost. Instead, they consider their profit a good (or great) return on that investment.

The key is setting the desired rate of return before the investment is made. Then, when the price reaches the previously-fixed level, there is no seller's remorse and no reason to regret the sale, even if the price increases.

If a producer doesn't use this system or doesn't want to sell because she believes the stocks or bonds will yield more profit and she has other assets to use for her skin in the game, there is no reason to sell. But if these are the only liquid assets the producer has, she may need to sell all of her holdings and forego potentially higher returns later.

The fourth Way is to use a whole life insurance policy for the initial cash investment.

Way 4: Your Insurance Policy

A whole life insurance policy has been called a "forced savings account" because of the cash value that builds over time as monthly payments are made to the insurance company.

This type of policy provides death benefits if the policyholder dies during the policy term. But while the policy is in effect, the owner can borrow funds against the discounted policy value at the interest rate stated in the contract.

Or, at the end of the policy term when the policy is fully paid, the holder can close it out and receive the cash value of the policy less any unpaid loans taken during the term.

Way 5 is selling your vehicle for your skin in the game for your movie.

Way 5: Your Vehicle

This Way involves selling a personal vehicle and investing the cash in a film. If a producer owns a car, truck, SUV or motorcycle that is fully-paid for, she can sell, refinance or pledge it as collateral against a loan.

If the producer is still making monthly payments but the car value is greater than the unpaid loan balance, she has a choice whether to sell it or seek other cash sources.

Another option is to sell an expensive vehicle and downsize to a cheaper one, retaining the profit for the film investment. Any one of these alternatives shows the producer's strong commitment to the film.

Way 6 to put your own skin in the game involves utilizing real estate that you own.

Way 6: Your Real Estate

Using real property that you own is the sixth Way to invest your cash in your film. You can monetize this real estate in one of two ways:

First, borrow against the equity in your real estate. If you are still paying a mortgage on the property but it is worth more than the purchase price, you could get a second mortgage against the equity or re-finance the home and get a new mortgage. The added value could have been created by increased property values or by paid-in equity on the mortgage. Or, if you own a property free and clear of any debt, lenders should be interested in making a mortgage loan against it based on an appraisal or other acceptable valuation.

Second, if the property is an investment that is less valuable to you than your film, you could sell the real estate and invest the proceeds in the film. Of course, if this is your family home or property held by your family for generations this might give you pause. In that case, revert to the first method to retain ownership of the property while pledging it for a home equity loan or mortgage you will eventually have to repay.

Either choice can be an excellent source of funds, subject to legal fees, bank closing costs, appraisal costs, and any broker commissions. These extra costs should be considered when deciding whether to use real estate as Way 6.

Way 7 is using a retirement fund.

Way 7: Your Retirement Fund

An older filmmaker with an employer 401(k), Individual Retirement Account or Roth IRA can use this Retirement Fund as Way 7.

She can borrow or withdraw cash from them. A financial professional should be consulted for specific restrictions, such as if the fund allows such loans, the age of the borrower, the amount to be borrowed, repayment requirements and other factors.

Penalties and taxes may be due on such loans. For example, a 10% early withdrawal penalty is due if the borrower is younger than a certain age, currently 59 1/2. Income taxes may be due on withdrawals, except for certain Roth IRA account withdrawals.

Before accessing a retirement fund, a producer should be able to withstand the loss of her entire investment. If the film makes its money back or generates a profit to repay her retirement fund, she is in an enviable position.

Ways 8-15 which follow involve donations and grants as sources of film financing.

10.

DONATIONS & GRANTS
WAYS 8-15 of 50

Way 8 looks at how your immediate circle of friends and family members can assist the funding process for your film. This Way raises film financing through gifts from "Friends & Family," often referred to as "F&F."

A. DONATIONS

Donations are gifts given to the producer for her film budget by contributors. These donors include family members, friends, angels, local companies, fiscal sponsors and agents and non-equity crowdfunding donors, all discussed hereafter in Ways 8 through 15.

Way 8: Friends & Family ("F&F")

No one knows better than a producer's close friends and family how much she believes in making her dream film a reality.

It is natural that a producer first asks for financial help from the people who know her best -- her friends and family. They are closest to her and have lived through her hopes for her dream project, sometimes for years.

So, if most filmmakers go to family and close friends first, what reaction are they likely to get? Depending on the family and the type of friends in a producer's close circle, a small amount of start-up funds is often possible. This usually happens after the producer first invests her own skin in the game.

When producers try to upset this apple cart and ask F&F for the first money in or for funds to cover the initial expenses, it is common to encounter resistance.

Family members and close friends are not typical film financiers. But if they see the producer's passion and hard-earned cash in the project, they are much more likely to donate to the project.

However, friends and family are similar to regular financiers in one regard. They will often balk at giving funds to a filmmaker who does not show her belief in her own project by investing her personal cash into the film.

Once you have put your own skin in the game and approached your F&F, Way 9 expands the circle of potential donors. These include work colleagues, friends' referrals and others who might donate to the production.

In addition to the tight-knit group of F&F and the expanded circle, producers should

FINANCING INDEPENDENT FILMS | 87

consider private donors and corporate and foundation grants.

Private donors are called angels, which is Way 9, below.

Way 9: Angel Donors

The angels in Way 9 are people who are not in the producer's F&F circle but who believe enough in the film to donate money to it.

This way does not involve selling any ownership interests to investors, since those are securities regulated by federal law. Equity ownership can only be offered or sold by the filmmaker in a securities offering registered with the SEC or exempt from registration, often using a private placement memorandum. Chapter 18 provides more information.

People who donate to your project outside your circle of family and friends are "angels." But they are not the same as "angel investors" who buy an equity stake in your film.

An angel donor who believes strongly in the film project may donate as well as referring the producer to other angels or his network. Angels also often lend funds with favorable repayment terms when profits are realized.

In addition to individual angel donors, local companies donate to films. This is Way 10.

Way 10: Local Company Donors

An additional means of obtaining financing for a film is Way 10, local company donors.

Although friends, family and angels often individually donate to a producer, she may overlook companies that take an active role in supporting arts in her community.

Large corporations generally have strict requirements, a formal application process and a highly-competitive system. Many local businesses donate in their communities though they have smaller budgets. These companies focus mainly on local causes, charities and non-profit organizations. Some companies do not donate to their local communities at all. Thus, the pool of potential donors in a producer's local area is much smaller than national corporations that have competitive procedures but fund throughout the country.

Local companies that donate to films often seek to make a difference in their city or county. Small to mid-sized local companies generally seek to enhance their community goodwill through donated funds. Donation amounts range from very small to generous and requirements vary from simple to complex.

The key to working with local businesses is to establish a rapport with the owners or managers and learn their "hot buttons" -- what their company mission or what the owners are passionate about. Show them how your film meets their company's need, perhaps even one they did not know existed. And always focus on the local publicity and positive public relations that the business will get for their donation.

In addition to including company donors in press releases and other public notices about the film, it is important to give them acknowledgements in the closing credits of the film. Also consider placing their company logo on film merchandise such as t-shirts and caps, giving on-set VIP tours to company executives, and other perks showing the production's appreciation of the company's support.

Include interviews with company managers and owners in the film's "behind-the-scenes" videos about why the film is important to them and the community. Customize a marketing package showing how the businesses will benefit from donations to the film. Keep the managers informed every step of the way during pre-production, production and post so they can see what efforts you are making that benefit them during this lengthy process.

Without requiring producers to go through a formal competitive process like grants, local company donors can provide extra financing at a time when it is really needed. However, this is not an overnight process. It takes research to determine what companies could benefit from being associated with your film.

The genre of your film may dictate which types of companies might be interested in being financial donors. A horror film could attract completely different businesses than a romantic comedy. Racy, edgy or violent films are generally a much more difficult sell than family-friendly films. Remember that local companies are seeking positive reactions, not controversy, from existing and potential customers in their local communities.

Giving interviews to local newspapers, radio stations, and morning shows on local television stations are all free advertisements for the film. Likewise, press releases and a strong social media campaign are extremely important. Any type of public outreach, publicity, promotion and advertisement available should always recognize and thank the local companies that donated to and supported the film.

Community interaction by the production company that co-brands the film and the donor company is a positive addition to a film's public relations campaign. For example, a producer could distribute t-shirts with the company logo and the film title throughout schools, community colleges or universities.

A sports-themed film could print the film and company logo on uniforms, caps or gym bags and provide them to local teams. A dance-related movie or a film about gymnastics could seek to tie-in with local dance companies, jazz groups, tumbling associations or ballet schools, depending on the theme. Christian and other religious-themed films could contact local churches, synagogues and other religious organizations for support.

Other possibilities for promotion are local news segments on television and radio. Or negotiate free on-air plugs with local radio deejays in exchange for film logo merchandise,

FINANCING INDEPENDENT FILMS | 91

on-set visits or a job as an extra in the film for radio contest giveaways.

If asked, a company donor might co-brand with the production by promoting the film in its ads, putting the film poster in windows, linking its website to the film website and other free advertising.

Local companies can also be a valuable resource for product or service placement or integration. These are explained in Chapter 11.

Another Way to raise funds for a film is through the use of fiscal sponsors and fiscal agents, explained in Way 11 below.

Way 11: Fiscal Sponsors & Agents

This section describes how a for-profit production company or producer can obtain access to film funding through the conduit of non-profit organizations. It is important to distinguish between two groups providing such access -- fiscal sponsors and fiscal agents.

Many donors only give financing for independent projects like films produced by IRS-approved tax-exempt organizations. Some examples are individuals, government entities, corporations and foundations.

Since most production companies are for-profit, they do not qualify for such funding opportunities. However, through the use of fiscal sponsors and fiscal agencies, independent films may be eligible to receive such funding.

Fiscal sponsorship is a legal and financial arrangement where tax-deductible donations are accepted by the tax-exempt sponsor of a for-profit company project. This is so even if the company is not tax-exempt pursuant to IRS Code Section 501(c)(3). But the project must be one that furthers the sponsor's own purpose.

The fiscal sponsor controls how and in what manner the funds are spent on the specific film project. This complete discretion and control over the donations assures that these financial resources are expended on the project to support or achieve the sponsor's objectives.

In contrast, fiscal agency is a fundraising opportunity where an established tax-exempt organization acts as a legal agent of the project. The agency can raise donations and grant them to the production company for the film.

A fiscal agent does not maintain control over the funding project as a fiscal sponsor does. Rather, the fiscal agent acts on behalf of the principal, i.e., the production company that controls and directs the agent's activities. However, donor contributions to a project with a fiscal agent are not tax deductible.

A tax-exempt entity or organization acting as a fiscal sponsor is the administrator for the film project. The sponsor accepts contributions from donors and issues them as grants to the production company to fund the film.

The fiscal sponsor can be any IRS-recognized legal non-profit or tax-exempt organization with which the producer or the film has a connection or proposes a project that benefits the sponsor as well.

The Internal Revenue Service has strict policies against using conduits for tax-deductible donations that do not meet the required criteria. Thus, before entering into any arrangements for donations to one entity (the fiscal agent or sponsor) for the use of another entity (the production company), it is important to contact a tax attorney or an accountant experienced in these matters before entering into any such arrangements.

Private foundations and other types of non-profit organizations are often restricted to granting funds only to IRS-recognized tax-exempt organizations. If this is the case, a fiscal sponsorship arrangement would not benefit a for-profit production company but would be an opportunity for a non-profit film company.

Local public television stations, activist groups, grassroots organizations, cause-related entities and many other types of non-profits could serve as the fiscal sponsor.

The relationship between a fiscal sponsor and a producer or production company can take different forms depending on the arrangement agreed to by the parties. This accord should be in writing and negotiated with the assistance of an attorney if the production company is not experienced in such financial structures and contracts.

Since the production company wishes to retain ownership of the film project, a grant agreement can be executed where the fiscal sponsor receives the contributions and, as a grantor, funds the production company as an independent contractor grantee. Tax attorneys and accountants can advise any grant tax consequences to the production company.

It is often helpful to start-ups and small production companies to work with a fiscal sponsor that handles back-office operations. Often, documentation and detailed reporting are required. Generally, the fiscal sponsor retains a modest fee or a small percentage of the donations that are received in exchange for administration of the grant.

The key to this type of film financing is understanding that the fiscal sponsor collects the donations and administers the grants to the production. Some fiscal sponsors require stringent oversight. Others may require regular reporting to receive the funding. Funding might be granted in parts over the period of the project, rather than prepaying in advance. Thus, the eleventh Way to raise financing for your film is through fiscal sponsors.

The twelfth Way is to utilize non-equity crowdfunding, explained below.

Way 12: Crowdfunding (non-equity)

By now, most producers are well-aware of online crowdfunding sites that facilitate raising funds for films. These donations are non-equity contributions, rather than sales of equity ownership in the films.

FINANCING INDEPENDENT FILMS | 95

Equity interests are securities that require registration or exemption therefrom. Now that the U.S. Securities & Exchange Commission ("SEC") has issued rules that are effective, numerous online portals are able to offer equity opportunities for investors to buy ownership interests in films and production companies. However, to comply with the law, such portals must be registered and meet the other criteria required by the SEC. Chapter 18 discusses this and other securities offering exemptions in Ways 47 through 50.

Rather than equity crowdfunding, Way 12 of 50 is the use of non-equity crowdfunding to raise film financing from a large number of crowdfunder donors who each contribute a small amount of funds.

Online crowdfunders donate to your film for any number of reasons. Perhaps they want to support you because you are a first-time producer, or because they like the story, genre or subject matter of the film. Their desire for an autographed movie poster or on-set visit may motivate them to donate. Crowdfunders can be inspired to donate by promotional material or a sizzle video or even how close the producer is to meeting her financial goal.

Regardless of the reasons why crowdfunders donate to a film, the method is a popular way to raise some financing early in development. The key to crowdfunding is to be reasonable, not greedy, with the amount requested. This is important due to the large number of film projects as well as non-film projects competing on such sites for funding.

Unless she is well-known, a producer faces greater challenges today to raise crowdfunding dollars. However, this form of online donating is still very important to a producer for numerous reasons.

First, crowdfunding sites are visited by millions of people. But even if your project does not achieve that number, you will be seen by many people who otherwise would not know about your film.

Second, if you set a reasonable target and reach or exceed it quickly, you may catch the attention of the crowdfunding site managers and become a featured "success story."

Third, visibility on crowdfunding sites gives a producer name recognition for her next project, if the first is successfully funded. Conversely, if the campaign is unsuccessful, the producer's credibility could be negatively impacted for future crowdfunding activities.

Fourth, if the financial goal for the movie is reasonable and donations reach or exceed that figure, the campaign will be successful and the producer can access the amount raised. If the amount raised is not reached, the filmmaker forfeits the right to use any of the funds raised, which are returned to the donors.

Fifth, a pitch for crowdfunding can be set up in phases. For example, the first amount could be raised for production, followed by another ask for post-production or finishing funds. The risk, of course, is that funds might not be raised for a phase, limiting production.

Sixth, a successful crowdfunding campaign can result in future film cash raises.

Ways 13-15 are grants from government agencies, corporations, non-profit foundations and non-profit organizations. Grants and these three Ways are discussed below.

B. GRANTS

Three main sources offering funding for projects through grants are government agencies (federal, state and local), corporations, and non-profit foundations and organizations.

Many grant opportunities are competitive, and often grants are offered to projects only in a narrow range of subjects. However, grant funds are not loans. Grants constitute free money, although as the adage says, "there ain't no free lunch." That means though the money is free, a time-consuming grant application and sometimes an application fee are required.

Ways 13, 14, and 15 to raise film financing are through grants from three different types of granting entities. The next section explains Way 13, government grants.

Way 13: Government Grants

The thirteenth Way to raise film financing is through government grants. Though the process is highly-competitive, substantial funding is distributed annually for films.

Two of these main government grant sources are the National Endowment for the Arts ("NEA") and the National Endowment for the Humanities ("NEH").

The NEA issues grants to media projects including film, audio, radio, television and online platform content. The NEH authorizes media grants for creative film, television and radio projects about humanities ideas in such disciplines as film studies, history, art history, literature, drama, religious studies, philosophy and anthropology.

The NEA and NEH federal budgets for each new fiscal year are subject to reduction or even elimination. Producers should research if final budgetary decisions have been made that affect grant availability and amounts.

The National Foundation on the Arts and the Humanities Act (1965), as amended, defines the term "humanities" as including:

> "...The study and interpretation of the following: language, both modern and classical; linguistics; literature; history; jurisprudence; philosophy; archaeology; comparative religion; ethics; the history, criticism and theory of the arts; those aspects of social sciences which have humanistic content and employ humanistic methods; and the study and application of the humanities to the human environment with particular attention to reflecting our diverse heritage, traditions, and history and to

the relevance of the humanities to the current conditions of national life."

This definition offers many opportunities for producers to express humanities in many unique and creative ways.

State, county and local governmental agencies and entities such as arts councils also provide grants to arts-related projects. Since each governmental entity is different, producers should research grant criteria in their local areas.

Way 14, corporate grants, is explained next.

Way 14: Corporate Grants

Many for-profit corporations provide cash grants in one of two ways. Either the company sponsors a foundation which is administered by the company, or the company has a corporate giving program. Their Community Relations or Corporate Social Responsibility department often reviews and issues the grants.

Besides grants, many corporations also match employee gifts and individual and team volunteer grants to employees who donate money, services or products to non-profits.

Companies that provide grants are found in industry sectors including:
- Airlines;
- Automobiles;
- Banks;
- Clothing/department stores;
- Communications;
- Entertainment;

- Food manufacturing;
- Fuel;
- Groceries;
- Hotel chains;
- Insurance;
- Mass/big box retail;
- Pharmaceuticals;
- Tech/Office; and
- Many others.

Producers should monitor corporate websites for grant criteria and deadlines to apply for their grants.

The fifteenth Way, below, is obtaining non-profit grants.

Way 15: Non-Profit Grants

In addition to corporate grants or employee matching funds, many corporations have created foundations that issue grants to non-profit companies. Way 15 is non-profit grants.

While most non-profit funding applications are for documentary submissions, some grants allow other types of films. If a producer wishes to make a socially-conscious film or documentary and support a social view, she should consider forming a non-profit production company. Such an organization can be eligible for lucrative grants awarded by corporate foundations each year.

Some of the granting organizations require fiscal sponsors while others issue grants to for-profit companies and individuals. Way 11 explains fiscal sponsors and fiscal agents, which could benefit producers and production companies.

Some grants are made on a matching basis, requiring the producer to raise the same amount as the grant before she receives it.

Before applying for a grant with any organization or fund, a producer should:
1. Read all the rules associated with the grant several times!
2. Verify if a fiscal sponsor or fiscal agent is required to apply for, or receive, a grant.
3. Review past grant project recipients.
4. Research the panel, board or individual who makes the decision and write your grant to appeal to their connection with your project.
5. Prepare the application elements well in advance. You might need third-party reference letters, a current director's reel, or other materials so plan ahead to have enough time to obtain them.
6. Take your time to complete the grant application, providing all the required elements in a legible, organized manner.
7. Be attentive to how your grant application looks. As a filmmaker, you want to capture the imagination, touch the heart, inspire creativity, or generate any of a myriad of possible emotional reactions from the reviewer.
8. Send the application ahead of the deadline. Notice if the deadline is a

"postmarked by" or "received by" date, which are not the same. NO LATE FILING!
9. Obtain proof of mailing your application by obtaining a tracking number, courier receipt or certified mail return receipt.
10. Once the grant has been turned in, stop thinking about it. You have submitted your application and nothing else can be done. Turn your energy toward your life, family, career and other projects with the confidence that you turned in your best. Now it is up to the grantor to make the decision, which often takes months.
11. Attend grant-making authority public hearings or meetings. In rare instances, city or county arts councils allow the public to attend (but not participate in) their meeting to discuss the grants before their final votes. Having attended such meetings and having won the grants, the author emphasizes the importance of showing decision-makers your passion and belief in your own application. Council members must make difficult decisions with many more applications than available funds. Taking the time to attend the meeting may make the difference in receiving a grant or not.

A list of some of the numerous corporate foundations that provide media grants are listed in Resources at the back of this book.

11.

PRODUCTS & SERVICES
Ways 16 – 22 of 50

Ways 16 through 22 describe how to access and utilize companies for discounted or free products and services, rather than grants. The sources of funding are vendors that provide products or services for props, consumables and departmental use. Film companies may also access these products and services through their integration or placement into a film.

Each of these Ways to "get the golden goose, not a goose egg" is listed separately to encourage producers to combine multiple Ways in their requests to companies.

The first set of Ways relates to products, which are Ways 16-18, as explained below.

A. PRODUCTS

An important thing to remember about consumable products needed by a production onscreen and off is they are line items in the budget that are usually purchased.

The good news about Ways 16, 17 and 18 is that often a production can obtain the products it needs without paying for them. In some cases, the production may be paid to use them in the film. These three ways are:
- Free products;
- Product Placement; and
- Product Integration.

A discussion follows on Way 16, obtaining free products for the production.

Way 16: Free Products

Way 16 is obtaining free consumables from companies that you need for the cast and crew. In other words, these are products the production uses off-screen during production.

Such products can include water and soft drinks, craft service items, catering food products and ingredients, clothing, logo merchandise, and so on -- virtually any type of product needed for a production cast and crew.

Products that are consumed and used by your cast and crew are a hefty part of any film production budget. Imagine if you could procure these products without having to pay for them:
- Food;
- Water;
- Soft drinks, energy drinks, etc.;
- Snacks/craft service items;

- Catering food and service ingredients, toppings, sauces, spices, etc.;
- Gas and oil;
- Office supplies;
- Printer and copier paper and supplies;
- Batteries;
- Clothing items and merchandise (t-shirts, caps) to brand with the film logo; and
- Many more products.

Major companies are bombarded with requests from independent filmmakers, so a producer should be reasonable in approaching manufacturers for free products.

However, a local or regional office or distributor might be willing to provide free products as part of their community goodwill, or for inviting their staff to the wrap party, or for screening the film at their offices.

Obtaining these consumables reduces the budget while increasing local or regional interest and free promotion for the film.

Way 17 goes beyond free products to include compensation to the production for Product Placement. This Way is explained hereafter.

Way 17: Product Placement

Some manufacturers pay a production fee to place their product onscreen, showing its use by a character in a logical way or as set decoration in the film. This is Way 17, Product Placement.

This method benefits a producer by saving the purchase or rental costs of the product or receiving added promotional consideration. Product placement can fit well in scenes with characters eating fast food, working out in shoes, buying clothing, filling a car with gas, buying or using office supplies, or drinking water, soda or alcohol, to name just a few.

If the product logically fits in the scene, any brand of these products will ring true since the particular brand is not integral to the story. But if an identifiable product or logo is shown, the manufacturer must give contractual approval.

Companies review the script and require approval of any onscreen use of their product and display of their brand. If the product is not depicted positively, producers should forego contacting companies for their products. The exception is if the company's brand identity allows "negative" product use.

Producers should use Product Placement as a means to reduce their budget wherever possible in the film. Integrating products into the storyline is Way 18, Product Integration.

Way 18: Product Integration

In Way 18, a branded product used in a scene is an indispensible part of telling the story. This is known as Product Integration, which improves a film budget in two ways:
- The producer receives free products if they seamlessly integrate them into the

script, thus saving the cost of props, rentals or other purchases; and
- The producer receives compensation from the product manufacturer for integrating the product into the storyline.

The product and brand must be a seamless part of the story and fit the manufacturer's brand image. Otherwise there is no reason for a company to allow its product to be in a film that is contrary to the company's brand identification and marketing story onscreen.

If any part of the integration is forced and is not truly woven into the storyline of the film, the audience will know it. This will detract greatly from both the integrity of the film and the product. In any such case, it is far better not to integrate the products than to do so and regret pushing them into the story and onto the screen.

Product manufacturers and distributors may also pay for Product Integration if the storyline meshes with their branding. Companies that do so may require strict script approval of the entire screenplay, not just the scenes in which their products are integrated.

An agreement with a supplier should include additional details such as which party will pay for product shipping, whether insurance is required and at whose cost, anticipated product delivery dates, ownership of excess or unused products, and other such specific terms.

Ways 19 and 20 involve services. Their explanations follow.

B. SERVICES

Ways 19 and 20 provide two new methods of accessing funding. These methods are procuring services needed for the production and integrating services into the film story in a logical way. These Ways are discussed in the pages that follow.

Way 19: Free Services

Way 19 is obtaining free services needed for a film at no cost from service providers. Way 19 is similar to Ways 16, 17, and 18, which result in the receipt of free products from companies that manufacture or distribute them.

The list of services that could be provided includes any that would be needed on set or for departments, cast and crew. The list of services required by a film is long, and usually includes the following industry sectors:
- Airlines;
- Art and artwork;
- Beauty (hair, make-up);
- Cleaning;
- Clothing alterations;
- Computers, cell phones and other tech;
- Furniture rentals;
- Lodging (long and short stay);
- Dry cleaning;
- Graphic design;
- Internet access;
- Limousine services;

FINANCING INDEPENDENT FILMS | 109

- Printing and copying;
- Rental vehicles;
- Signage;
- Trash pick-up; and
- Many other services.

Such providers may also contribute to the budget if their services are integrated in a meaningful way into the film.

Way 20: Service Integration

What producer would not want to get free services and compensation when using those services as part of the storyline? Way 20 is this method, Service Integration.

Often a screenplay is set in a service-provider business -- car wash, beauty salon, dry cleaner, restaurant, retailer, hotel and many others. If a producer contacts the service provider well in advance of production, the provider may be willing to provide free services and a free shooting location for integrating the brand in the film.

Such service providers generally place many restrictions on the film, including approvals of onscreen brand identity and script changes, as their brand identity is at risk. Some businesses providing services include:

- Airlines, helicopter firms, charter firms, drone companies, and hot air balloons;
- Apparel stylists;
- Accessory, shoe and jewelry stylists;

- Beauty consultants, hair stylists and make-up artists;
- Dry cleaners, laundries and alteration shops;
- Hotels, motels and apartments;
- Nightclubs, discos, private clubs, bars, karaoke spots, and other dance clubs;
- Rental car companies;
- Restaurants, cafes and fast food spots; and
- Taxis and self-owned vehicles.

While the above list is not complete, a producer can obtain other services for a film by determining the type or category of service needed and pitching the companies that provide it.

C. RENTALS

Ways 21 and 22 are methods in which suppliers, vendors and manufacturers provide filmmakers with free or discounted production rentals in exchange for integrating their products and brand logos into the film.

These two Ways are described below.

Way 21: Free Rentals

Way 21 is obtaining the use of free rentals from manufacturers, distributors or local companies, similar to Way 19 for free services. These rentals can include:

- Equipment for departments:

- Camera;
- Sound;
- Lighting;
- Editing;
- Transportation; and
- Other departments;
• Office Equipment:
  - Computers;
  - Phones;
  - Fax machines; and
  - Other office equipment;
• Property:
  - Consumable props; and
  - Non-consumable props;
• Costumes & Wardrobe:
  - Period costumes;
  - Contemporary costumes;
  - Uniforms;
  - Shoes; and
  - Hats, bags, belts and other accessories.

Rentals of items for a production constitute an important part of the budget, so free rentals reduce the budget substantially. To obtain the rentals, a producer should provide a package offering benefits and advantages to a resource such as a distributor or rental house.

As explained in other Ways, the vendor and the production company should enter into a written agreement specifying their mutual obligations. As with paid rentals, the supplier will usually ask to be included as a loss payee on the production insurance policy. This is security for the company to receive the rent-free items returned in good condition without damage.

Other terms such as shipping or delivery costs to and from the production, and onscreen visibility and credits should also be covered in the agreement.

Another opportunity for a producer or filmmaker to make the budget by reducing costs is by obtaining a discount on rentals. This is Way 22, below.

Way 22: Discounted Rentals

How beneficial is it to a producer to obtain discounts on rentals of equipment and other property needed for a production? Way 22 is using discounted rentals to reduce the financing needed for a budget.

When a producer calculates the cost of rentals for various departments (camera, sound, lighting, editing, transportation and others), office equipment rentals (computers, phones, fax machines and other types of equipment), props (consumable and non-consumable), rental costumes and wardrobe clothing, shoes and accessories, the total is surprising.

What if that cost could be cut by 10%, 25%, or even half? Think of how much that discount is worth. While it means bottom-line savings, it also reduces the budget and amount of financing needed to greenlight the film.

To implement this Way, make a list of the equipment, props, costumes and other items the production needs to rent. Then verify if the story can still meet the director's vision while integrating and displaying products and company logos onscreen.

If these visuals are natural to the story or if the screenplay can be easily adapted to include them, the producer could benefit from rental discounts on those necessary items.

What kinds of businesses provide services to a producer? The numerous categories include:
- Airlines, helicopter firms, charter firms, drone companies, and hot air balloons;
- Apparel stylists;
- Accessory, shoe and jewelry stylists;
- Beauty consultants, hair stylists and make-up artists;
- Dry cleaners, laundries and alteration shops;
- Hotels, motels and apartments;
- Nightclubs, discos, private clubs, bars, karaoke spots, and other dance clubs;
- Rental car companies;
- Restaurants, cafes and fast food spots; and
- Taxis and self-owned vehicles.

While the above list is not complete, it is easy to add other types of service providers by simply determining the service essential to producing a film and finding providers for it.

The next Chapter discusses six additional Ways of the 50 Ways to make or reduce your production budget.

These Ways involve the participation of above-the-line creatives like producers, directors and key cast, while also including below-the-line crew. These six Ways offer methods showing how team effort of those working on or attached to a film can help bring the budget to fruition and make the project a reality.

12.

TEAM EFFORT
Ways 23 - 28 of 50

    Filmmaking has been referred to as a family sport. Long working hours, a common goal, and a looming deadline all contribute to cast and crew acting as a team, like a family, to achieve their mutual objective.

    As the old saying goes, "It takes a village" to get a job done. Making an independent film is no different. Everyone who works on a production, whether above- or below-the-line, whether cast or crew, whether producer, writer or director, must ultimately come together as a team to make the project successful.

    It makes sense that a producer should embrace the idea of getting financing, or budget reduction, from the other members of the team. That does not usually translate into actual cash loans, but rather to other Ways, including deferrals and back-end profit participations for delays or reductions in compensation.

Ways 23 through 28 provide six new Ways to make the budget. These Ways reduce the need for immediate cash on certain line items through deferrals and back-end participation in profit-sharing. These are paid once the film has been completed and revenues are generated or funds for these purposes have been obtained.

Certain production companies that are union signatories generally cannot use these Ways. This is so because some union cast and crew compensation terms are established by contracts. These unions include the Director's Guild of America ("DGA") for directors, first assistant directors and like positions; SAG-AFTRA for cast; and IATSE for certain crew.

The Producers Guild of America ("PGA") does not require or restrict compensation to producers and producer positions. Producer contracts are freely negotiable between the parties. Because of this fact, producers are often amenable to deferring some or all of their compensation in exchange for a percentage participation in film profits, or the increase of an existing back-end.

However, producers of non-union films can and should access as many of these Ways as possible.

The interesting thing about these Ways is that it generally only requires the producer to ask and she shall receive.

The cast and crew "family" members are usually so passionate about the indie film in which they are involved that they are willing to put their money (literally) where their mouths are. Producers can then make agreements with them to defer, reduce, or exchange their compensation for back-end profit participation to finalize the budget and make the film.

Ways 23 through 27 discuss how to lower the budget and require less cash for production by obtaining deferrals. Way 28 discusses back-end, as explained hereinafter.

A. DEFERRALS

This Chapter provides a valuable tool to help producers make their budget – deferrals. To defer is to delay. Thus, a "deferral" is an agreement between the production company and certain members of the cast or crew to delay certain line item payments.

Deferrals often delay payment of production compensation until sufficient revenues are generated through distribution or other sources. Deferrals should always be in writing, determine when the postponed compensation or other line item will be paid and specify the order of deferral repayment relative to lenders and investors.

Ways 23, 24, 25, 26 and 27 cover costs in the budget by deferrals.

Way 23: Producer Deferrals

Way 23 is an obvious Way to finance a film by deferring all or part of the producer's fee.

This may be a tough pill to swallow for independent producers who have already invested skin in the game. However, two questions should be answered before deciding:
1. Will my film only be made if I defer my compensation until the film starts to make money?
2. Can I survive/pay my bills/eat if I don't get paid during production?

If a producer answers "yes" to both of these questions, it should be a no-brainer. This is true even if is not the ideal decision since everyone wants to be paid when they work.

In the end, this decision depends on whether the producer believes strongly enough that the film will make money. She must be willing to risk that she will not get paid at all unless the film generates sufficient revenues.

On the other hand, consider what will happen if the producer fails to raise the money needed for the budget, and the film is not made. In that case, the producer does not get paid for her effort during development or for her skin in the game she invested into the film.

So, the decision is ultimately up to each producer. Those who are confident in their story, their skills, their cast and their crew will almost always be willing to defer their payments until the film makes enough money.

Some producers may find these too difficult, because of family situations or personal obligations. In these cases, producers could consider a partial deferral. This would

FINANCING INDEPENDENT FILMS | 119

allow some of their budgeted compensation to be delayed until the film begins to generate revenues. There is an upside for a producer with a partial deferral. She is not placed under an undue hardship and is still able to take care of family finances or personal needs.

Additional benefits are also usually given to producers who are not owners of the production company in the form of back-end participation. This is discussed in Way 28.

The next method, Way 24, is deferring compensation of the director of the film.

Way 24: Director Deferrals

After Way 23, in which film producers agree to delay receipt of their compensation, the next most common method of this type is Way 24, director deferrals.

An experienced director who is passionate about the project and yearns for another director credit is a likely candidate to delay some or all of his compensation until the film starts generating revenues.

If the director is a first-timer, his appetite for compensation deferral may be greater than a director of prior movies. Often a first credit is too important to a director to let payment of his full compensation block the opportunity.

If the director is committed to substantial personal or family financial obligations that require payment, deferral of the entire fee may not be a viable option. In this case, delaying part of the compensation till the film starts earning revenues might be an acceptable alternative to the director.

A multi-hyphenate such as a writer-director or actor-director has higher stakes in the film than others and is a prime candidate for a deferral. Of course, if the director is also the producer, he has the ultimate obligation to raise enough money, cut the budget or defer as much as necessary to make the film.

As mentioned in Way 23, films produced pursuant to guild signatory contracts will not generally be able to use this Way. DGA contracts control how and when compensation is to be paid to a DGA director or other position covered by this guild.

Notwithstanding these issues, some indie directors may be willing to defer part or all of their compensation. In turn, this will reduce the budget and require less film financing.

Way 25 is deferring cast compensation.

Way 25: Cast Deferrals

In addition to Ways 23 and 24, in which producers and directors agree to defer part or all of their compensation until the film is completed and exploited, cast members may also agree to such deferrals.

A cast member who is willing to defer his compensation until the movie earns revenues is a person who is truly passionate about the film. Lead and supporting actors may surprise a producer in their willingness to accept deferred payments.

If first-time or new actors are cast to star in an independent film, a producer may ask them to defer compensation to get the movie made. This could be a delay of part or all of their salary. Often the first or early credits are so important that the actors are willing to assist the producer. They help reduce production cash needs in order to jump-start their career.

This is not to say that a producer will always get agreement from the entire cast. Day players and extras may make too little to agree to deferred compensation. Or, they and other cast members may be unpaid volunteers.

A producer should focus on key actors with the largest parts in the film. The more their participation is crucial to the story, the more a producer should try to negotiate a deferral.

As seen in Ways 23 and 24, if a production company is a signatory to a union and makes a union film, this deferral measure is not available. SAG-AFTRA requires that signatory production companies must comply with the terms of their guild agreement, including compensation payment and timing terms.

Many actors and actresses who are passionate about the screenplay and their characters may agree to a deferral, but usually have certain conditions. These might include a production credit like co-executive producer, executive producer, co-producer or producer. In essence, their agreement to delay receipt of their compensation partially funds the film which is a producer's role.

Another demand might be to pay their agent's commission in full at the start of principal photography, or on the terms originally negotiated in the talent agreement.

If an agent has been an integral participant in bringing cast to the movie, the agent might consider a deferral with a production credit, so long as his client(s) and the agency also agree.

Way 26: Crew Deferrals

The foregoing three Ways explain deferring compensation for certain producer, director and cast members on the film. Likewise, other members of the crew might also agree to a deferral. This is Way 26, crew deferrals.

Crew members who are department heads may agree to a deferral of some or all of their compensation. Likewise, crew members who are getting a credit opportunity or are hired in a higher position than their usual job might also be willing to defer at least some pay.

It would be highly unusual to defer all crew payments. In some cases, the crew is already working for little to no pay at all, perhaps just for meals. But paid crew who will earn their first credit might be willing to defer some or all of their compensation to make the film and receive their credit. That is their own skin in the game. They cannot move their career forward until they get their first or another valuable credit.

Way 27 is deferring above-the-line pay.

Way 27: Other Above-the-Line Deferrals

After deferrals for producer, director, cast and crew, potential still exists for deferrals for other above-the-line creative team members.

For instance, the screenwriter of a film could agree to defer compensation to get the film made. He may negotiate additional credits such as producer or executive producer.

Other above-the-line professionals might defer pay for an upgraded credit, better credit placement, single cards, and other benefits.

Sometimes a deferral can result in increased compensation when it is finally paid. The logic behind an increase is that the person deferring payment risks not being paid at all if the film does not generate sufficient revenues. Extra risk deserves the added reward in the form of more money.

It is the producer's responsibility to raise the financing necessary for a film. This can be achieved only by obtaining all funding needed or by obtaining part of the budget and reducing the remainder through discounts, donations, and deferrals to a later date.

The more successful the producer is in obtaining agreements for deferrals, the quicker the production can start since it requires raising less money.

Way 28 reduces the budget by lowering compensation in exchange for back-end profit participation. This is explained in the following section.

B. BACK-END

Often a producer can lower the need for immediate cash funding for a film by granting a profit participation on the "back-end" to cast and crew that reduce their compensation.

Way 28: Reduced Compensation for Back-End Profit Participation

In Way 28, a cast or crew member cuts his compensation for a small percentage of the profits. Lead actors, the director, or other above-the-line team members may choose to accept a lower salary for a back-end.

An indie film screenwriter may accept a lower writing fee or script purchase price for a back-end participation. This would not apply to Writer's Guild of America ("WGA") members since the WGA contract requires minimum payments for writing services and screenplays.

A back-end percentage is not ownership equity in the film but a percentage of the profits generated by the movie after certain obligations are paid.

Payment of the back-end is contingent on repayment of all debt and deferrals. Back-end participations are paid on a "pari-passu" basis, without partiality. This means the back-end recipients receive their profit shares at the same time as the producer does.

13.

LOCATIONS
Ways 29-30 of 50

Every film needs locations, whether the interior of a house or building or an exterior shoot on a street, in a park, on a mountain, or any of thousands of other potential sites.

The information in this Chapter offers two ways to make or lower your location expense which is often a significant budget item. Savvy producers and filmmakers use every tool available to reduce location fees. These include obtaining locations at no charge or for a discounted fee, which are Ways 29 and 30.

Way 29: Free Locations

This method of making a budget is negotiating fee waivers to get free locations. By using Way 29, producers can reduce the amount of funds needed for the film.

A location fee waiver agreement is a modified version of a standard location agreement typically used by producers, location managers and line producers. A waiver means that there is no fee to utilize the location.

In the typical location agreement the price would be specified as "Waived/No Charge." However, an insurance policy rider naming the owner is usually required to protect the property owner against damage and liability.

In underutilized locations used in films such as rural settings, small towns, out-of-the-way places and rarely-seen spots, location owners often get excited about having a film made in their home, business or community.

In these cases, producers have a valuable opportunity to negotiate no-cost or low-cost locations with homeowners, business owners and local government leaders.

In cities, counties and regions with a film commission, a producer often receives free services. Before a scout, producers should contact the local film commission about perks offered in that area.

A recent survey of film commissions found offers of free local scouts and transportation, free or discounted local lodging, sponsored meals, free location photos, a "red-tape" liaison staffer to streamline the process of permits and other legal requirements, and discounts with local vendors. Speaking with the film commissioner in advance of a potential scouting trip may yield additional incentives not listed on the commission website.

Many countries and U.S. cities, counties and states are members of the Association of Film Commissioners International ("AFCI"). This organization can be a useful resource for producers before they scout locations. About 300 AFCI members on six continents provide a variety of services. The website is www.afci.org.

It is highly recommended for producers to give a thank-you gift to property owners who allow filming on their property at no charge. This could be an official film poster signed by the cast members, producer and director. Or it could be film logo merchandise for the family or owner of the location where the film was shot. Invitations to the wrap party are always welcome gifts.

Verify the jurisdiction's laws before giving thank-you gifts to local officials, due to legal limits on gifts, meals or other items of value. If gifts are not allowed, giving film ending credits if allowed and thank-you notes to government staff are always appreciated.

Way 30, discounted locations, follows.

Way 30: Discounted Locations

By utilizing Way 30, producers can reduce their location budget with discounted fees for certain locations.

It always pays to negotiate location fees with private property owners. They will often consider discounting their location fees for rental periods longer than a few days. Local, state and federal government locations are generally offered at a low fixed rate. Additionally, many provide discounts to non-profit production companies. Some public locations could be free, discussed in Way 29.

Government and public locations include:
- Colleges and schools;
- Convention centers;
- Courthouses;
- Government buildings;
- Libraries;
- Museums;
- Training centers;
- Parks;
- Rivers, lakes, ponds, bayous and other public bodies of water;
- Sports fields and stadiums (licensing fees may be charged to film any sponsor signage and team or school logo); and
- Streets, highways and alleys (fees are often charged for police, fire and security).

The key to obtaining discounted or low-fee locations is to request them several months in advance and attempt to negotiate lower rates for more production days. A standard location agreement is used for Way 30, with the discounted price being the location fee. The contract also lists insurance rider requirements that producers must fulfill.

Using Ways 29 and 30 for free or discounted locations during production will help make or reduce the budget for producers and filmmakers.

14.

SOFT MONEY 1: REBATES & EXEMPTIONS
Ways 31-34 of 50

Soft money incentives are offered by many jurisdictions to attract producers. Soft money is not cash but it is "free money." Soft money incentives include rebates, exemptions and tax credits that reduce the budget. Of the many benefits of such incentives, the most important is that they do not require repayment. This is why soft money is referred to as "free money."

Local, city, county and state governmental authorities often offer incentives such as sales tax rebates on local purchases or refunds or exemptions from lodging taxes, depending on the number of nights stayed.

Tax credits issued to a film based on the film's expenditures in the jurisdiction are also soft money. These are discussed in Chapter 15.

Lodging and sales tax incentives are Ways 31-34, below.

A. LODGING INCENTIVES

Many jurisdictions offer rebates or waivers on sales taxes on lodging or on local purchases and rentals. Way 31 is a lodging tax rebate.

Way 31: Lodging Tax Rebates

Way 31 is a direct reduction of the budget line item for accommodations. The reduction is realized through Lodging Tax Rebates issued by governmental authorities.

Usually a city, county or state charges a daily add-on tax to lodging such as hotels, motels, B&B's and short-stay facilities. Many offer a direct rebate to productions that occupy lodging for 30 days or more. After that, it becomes long-term housing like apartments, on which typically no lodging tax is charged.

Producers should verify with the local jurisdiction all available incentives and the paperwork to access and track such rebates during production. Supporting hotel or motel receipts with cost and tax breakdowns are usually required to obtain these rebates.

Rebate checks are generally issued by the jurisdiction after the required length of time of the stay and the expenses have been verified.

Way 32 is a lodging tax exemption.

Way 32: Lodging Tax Exemptions

Way 32, lodging tax exemptions, is like Way 31 except better! Instead of a production paying lodging taxes on location, many jurisdictions grant immediate exemptions from paying the taxes at all. This means Way 32 is an immediate reduction of the budget.

Since each city, county, state and foreign location is different, it is up to the producer or assigned production team member to research the incentives offered and to take advantage of all for which the film qualifies.

With a lodging tax rebate, money is paid from the budget for the taxes, which are later refunded. But a tax exemption does not require payment at all. However, a jurisdiction may require advance registration of the production to qualify for incentives, and later verification of receipts to justify them.

No matter how a governmental jurisdiction decides to offer incentives, astute producers and filmmakers take advantage of them all.

Ways 33 and 34 are similar to Ways 31 and 32 but relate to sales tax rebates and exemptions, rather than to lodging tax incentives. These Ways are found below.

B. SALES TAX INCENTIVES

Another important way to reduce the budget for a film is a rebate or exemption of sales taxes on purchases for the film.

If some or all of the purchases needed for a film can be made in the jurisdiction, these two Ways -- sales tax rebates and exemptions -- could result in substantial savings.

Accessing these incentives reduces the financing needed for the production. Ways 33 and 34 are discussed in the pages that follow.

Way 33: Sales Tax Rebates

A direct deduction of multiple budget line items is Way 33, rebates of sales taxes paid to a jurisdiction on production purchases.

Producers have an opportunity to reduce the budget through simple research. Verify with a city or county tax office or local film commission as to the policy on sales taxes for production purchases and rentals.

It may surprise filmmakers to know that many of these jurisdictions offer rebates on sales taxes if production purchases and rentals are made within their geographic taxing area.

Consider how quickly the total adds up for line items for "Purchases" and "Rentals" in each department. It only makes good financial sense to take advantage of sales tax rebates offered by an authority, rather than buying or renting items outside that jurisdiction.

Rebates of sales taxes are payments issued by the taxing jurisdiction to the production company after verifying purchases and rentals made within the taxing area.

A producer should obtain the paperwork prior to commencing any work in the chosen location. The application is generally simple but requires details of all purchases and rentals and supporting documentation such as receipts and rental agreements.

FINANCING INDEPENDENT FILMS | 133

Different jurisdictions may require different types of reviews. At a minimum, the store name, location, date, and amount of the purchase or rental and relevant sales tax should be legible on the receipts. Otherwise, the receipt may be challenged or disallowed as not meeting the criteria for the incentive.

By obtaining the requirements in advance for expenditures in the area, a producer can complete the paperwork during production as purchases or rentals or made, or shortly thereafter. This eliminates wading through myriads of expenditures to find qualifying expenses after the production wraps.

The production accountant or person charged with this responsibility can easily track and record expenses in real time when incurred. An entertainment or accounting software program will streamline this process.

The taxing entity will generally issue a rebate check within a reasonable period after the required documentation is submitted. The rebate procedure may offer additional rebates for future expenditures, such as marketing, post-production, and promotion of the film.

An even better method to reduce the budget is through sales tax exemptions where the tax is never paid at all. This means no delay in waiting for a rebate check. Way 34 follows.

Way 34: Sales Tax Exemptions

A sales tax exemption, Way 34, is similar to Way 33 except it does not require the outlay of cash for taxes when purchases or rentals are made.

Rather than charging taxes on these items for a production, many governmental jurisdictions will grant exemptions from paying the tax in the first place.

By not having to pay sales taxes on items purchased or rented for the production, the producer can re-allocate the sales taxes budget line item for use elsewhere on the production.

This means a producer does not have to pay this line item from the budget then wait to receive a rebate check after the production has wrapped and the producer has moved on.

Regulations are different in cities, counties, states and foreign locations. The producer or assigned production team member should research the incentives and fiscal benefits offered to films in each jurisdiction.

To access incentives, a jurisdiction usually requires the pre-registration of the film with the estimated budget and other information about anticipated expenses. It may also require a post-production accounting audit to verify paid receipts.

But no matter what process and procedures a governmental authority requires before a film can qualify for and access incentives, knowledgeable producers and filmmakers make an effort to take advantage of them all.

The following Ways 35 and 36 relate to tax credits and include rebates and sales of incentives issued by governmental authorities.

15.

SOFT MONEY 2: TAX CREDITS
Ways 35-36 of 50

In addition to rebates and exemptions, an often-overlooked source of soft money is the tax credit incentive in certain U.S. states and foreign locations. Producers are enticed to spend money in their locales on production, labor and talent in exchange for tax credits equal to a percentage of those expenditures.

State tax credits reduce the individual and/or corporate income tax in the jurisdiction where they are issued. However, a production filmed on location generally cannot use the tax credits because it does not generate taxable income in that state. In this case, the production must find buyers for the credits.

Sometimes states offer direct rebates for the credits which are paid to the production after completion. If not rebated, producers sell the tax credits to taxpayers. In some locales, tax credit brokers act as middlemen between the production and taxpayers to sell the credits.

SOFT MONEY 2: TAX CREDITS

Ways 35 and 36 below provide methods of using tax credits as valuable sources of free money for film financing.

Way 35: Tax Credit Rebates

Way 35 is the use of tax credit rebates as a source of free film funding. To earn tax credits from city, county, state or foreign jurisdictions a film usually must be pre-qualified, or pre-certified.

Later, after the production expenditures are paid the accounts are audited, if required for verification. Thereafter, the issuing tax credit authority releases the rebate payment to the production company for the tax credits earned.

For many films, this funding is necessary to pay for post-production, marketing, Prints & Advertising ("P&A"), festival fees, cast and crew deferrals or other expense items required to complete, promote and exploit the film.

Way 36 explains tax credit sales in jurisdictions where a certificate, not a rebate, for the tax credits is issued to the production.

Way 36: Tax Credit Sales

While Way 35 is a tax credit rebate payment from the jurisdiction, Way 36 is the sale of tax credits to local taxpayers for cash.

It is important for producers to verify what type of tax credit regime a governmental authority uses. Many authorities require pre-certification of the production before pre-

FINANCING INDEPENDENT FILMS | 137

production or filming, followed by an accounting audit after the film is completed.

The general requirements for pre-certifying the production vary from one jurisdiction to another. Generally, they include an application with information such as the final script, budget, production team, director, cast, locations, shooting days, estimated number of local hires and more.

Some states also require that a local bank account be opened to pay and track the expenditures made in the state. Many also require a production company to be formed in the state to earn tax credits. Others grant tax credits to out-of-state production companies that spend production dollars in their area.

The producer can apply for final certification of tax credits after all expenditures have been made.

Often an accounting audit of the expenses is required, usually by a third-party accountant or the jurisdiction's auditor. The audit determines the expenses qualified to earn tax credits. Approval or denial can take several weeks or even months.

Upon approval, the production company receives an official certification confirming the total value of the tax credits earned.

The tax credits must be transferable in order to sell them and obtain cash for the production. This means that the production can transfer, or sell, the credits to taxpayers who have a state tax liability. In many states, middlemen known as "tax credit brokers" buy the tax credits from the production at a substantial discount.

The brokers then sell the credits to in-state taxpayers at a much higher price, pocketing a hefty spread. Taxpayers are willing to buy the credits because the producer or broker will sell them at a slight discount.

After filing the application with the appropriate authority and receiving pre-approval, the production company produces the film. Often an accounting audit of all qualified expenses is required. Sometimes the state or jurisdiction will perform the audit for a fee. Otherwise, an outside audit may be done by a qualified accountant or firm.

The jurisdiction approves or disallows expenses according to its statutes and regulations, then issues a tax credit certification to the producer. The producer can apply the earned tax credits to any state tax owed. If the production owes no taxes, the credits are sold.

Some states restrict transfers of tax credits to reduce corporate income tax only, which limits buyers to in-state corporations.

Other states allow only one resale. This eliminates broker sales and requires producers to find local taxpayers to buy the credits.

Fortunately, many states allow multiple tax credit sale transfers. The first transfer is from the production to a taxpayer buyer or tax credit broker. Then the next transfer is from the buyer or broker to another buyer.

At each transfer, the buyer sells for a higher price than he paid and makes a profit. The production receives a discounted amount for the tax credits. This can be used to augment the budget, repay loans or reimburse investors, pursuant to the financing documents.

The tax credit process may seem complicated but it is worth the effort. The projected planned in-state expenditures should be based on the final budget since some jurisdictions do not grant tax credits on any budget increases after filing an application.

Sometime a production can borrow against tax credits to finance the production. Loan advances using future earned tax credits as collateral can be used. This is discussed in Chapter 16, which details various types of debt.

Ways 37 and 38, which follow, discuss film financing by pre-sales into foreign territories.

16.

PRE-SALES
Ways 37-38 of 50

Ways 37 and 38 are two additional methods of raising film financing by selling foreign film rights in international territories.

Way 37 involves obtaining loans against estimates of international sales from a Foreign Sales Agent acceptable to the lender. Way 38 consists of pre-sales to buyers in international territories, either directly or through a Foreign Sales Agent or Distributor.

These two Ways are discussed below, starting with Way 37, foreign sales estimates.

Way 37: Foreign Sales Estimates

Another method of obtaining film financing is Way 37. This method is obtaining loans based on foreign sales estimates of the film by reputable Foreign Sales Agents ("FSA's").

Entertainment financiers often lend funds using as collateral their professional estimates of film sales prices in foreign territories, referred to as foreign sales.

The FSA that estimates the film's foreign sales must be acceptable to the lender, who has often worked with the agent before or knows the agent to be accurate and reputable. Third-party insurers may be required to insure the sales, reducing the lender's risk.

FSA's that are well-known and acceptable to an entertainment lender may provide a "Minimum Guarantee" ("MG") of estimated potential revenues for the film in certain territories. This Way generates film financing for producers from loans against reputable sales estimates by experienced FSA's for the film in foreign territories.

The FSA typically underestimates foreign sales, because he puts his reputation on the line. He must surpass the estimates to maintain producer business and lender credibility.

Insurers generally guarantee less than the total sales estimates. These companies always want to hedge any losses if foreign sales are grossly underestimated or the market changes.

The lender considers the experience of the insurer and the FSA before lending against the estimates which are the collateral to induce the bank to make the loan. The bank must anticipate revenues of at least the amount of the estimates prior to lending against them.

The lender will hold the insured estimates as collateral but will not grant a 100% loan against them. By doing so, the bank hedges its risk position for sales overestimations or the failure of the insurer to cover its commitment.

Way 38: Foreign Pre-Sales

The next method of obtaining film financing is Way 38, foreign pre-sales of a film. These are actual or guaranteed revenues by an FSA for the sale of a film into international territories before completion.

The FSA can become a producer's new best friend. While some distributors offer to sell a film both domestically and internationally, a producer should consider FSA's specializing only in international sales.

This is an important consideration since film demands continuously change in foreign markets just as in the United States. For example, this year a foreign film purchaser may demand thriller movies. But next year, the same buyer may buy only horror films, or action features. Similarly, certain actors or directors may be "in" now and "out" next year.

FSA's spend years to build, maintain and expand international buyer networks and to keep their finger on the pulse of buyer demand. They invest in sales booths and screenings at major international film markets and pre-promote films to potential buyers. These activities offer strong opportunities for foreign pre-sales in many territories as quickly as possible after the film is announced or released.

A film pre-sale during development or pre-production is generally unlikely unless name cast or a known director is attached, or the film genre is in-demand. But film pre-sales can be made by buyers on any basis, even a unique movie poster or catchy title!

Film markets, often held during major international film festivals, are the best place for pre-sales. Even without being selected for an official screening, a film can be seen by buyers in private screenings arranged by the FSA. FSA's may also provide viewing stations in a sales booth or in market-provided facilities for buyers to see films without leaving the market or spending time in a theatre.

There are always exceptions to individual viewings such as world premieres, films with substantial buzz or an in-demand movie on a distributor's "hot list" for his territory.

FSA's and distributors offer thousands of films at each market. But most independent film buyers usually do not have time to watch the entire film at a market which only lasts from a few days to about two weeks. An impressive first ten minutes and a twist in the third act or ending may be enough to sell it.

Sometimes a film trailer, the film poster or promotional materials motivate the buyer to request a screener or digital link to view the film at home. The title and key art, as much as the content, should make the film memorable to attract buyers. Otherwise, the film may end up like many other films that are mediocre, ignored, or quickly forgotten rather than sold.

    FSA's typically propose "standard" contracts deducting sales commissions and tens or hundreds of thousands of dollars of nebulous "marketing expenses" from potential revenues which might result in little to no income to the producer. The producer may wish to engage an entertainment attorney with distribution experience to negotiate more favorable terms for the producer in such FSA contracts.

    With a major A-lister heading the cast, an FSA will spend more on marketing than for an unknown cast. However, even then, he might not spend all the "standard" expenses that he bills the producer. For no-name talent films, the agent usually does not spend much to promote the film, if at all. But he still pockets the advance or deducts standard expenses and fees before paying a producer from film sales.

    If the FSA has no prior sales in the same genre of film as the producer's movie, she should question putting her baby in the hands of an inexperienced person. Consider the best person to sell a high-priced Manhattan apartment with a Central Park view. Would it be an agent who leases apartments? One who sells studio condos? Or do you choose an agent who specializes in selling multi-million-dollar apartments?

    Likewise, think of what you would do if you wanted to sell a classic convertible. Would you take it to a used car lot? Or would you entrust your vehicle to a dealer who specializes in classic cars and works with clientele in that market?

The obvious choice is the person with experience in selling similar properties and knowledge of the buyers in the market. Likewise, these are the minimum requirements to consider in choosing the right salesperson for your film. If you believe in your film and its market, then surely the most experienced FSA *for your type of film* is the one to hire.

Remember that the best Foreign Sales Agent *for your film* may not always be the largest company. Successful agencies handling big-budget films or festival winners may not be the right fit for an indie or genre film. It is important to research and interview FSA's to determine the best fit for your film.

Other Chapters in this book provide information on related topics. For example, different types of marketing professionals are described in Chapter 7. And Chapter 20 provides different methods of distribution.

Chapter 17 explains different ways to obtain and utilize debt to finance a film. Debt may not always be the best, or the least expensive, source of film financing. Many producers may not qualify for film loans. However, debt is another series of Ways in the toolbox of film financing that is worthwhile to learn and to access when necessary and available.

Ways 39 through 45 about debt as a method of film financing are discussed next.

17.

DEBT
Ways 39-45 of 50

For most producers, "debt" is a dirty word. They don't want to think about it. Instead, they hope and pray that their dream will come true on "OPM" ("Other People's Money") that does not require repayment.

Obviously, free money is the best way to fund a film if a producer can obtain it. This includes donations, grants, sponsorships, tax credits, deferrals, product integration, pre-sales or any of the other Ways already discussed.

But sometimes that still is not enough to make the budget. In this case, a producer can consider debt from financiers who will loan the money to make the film a reality.

A filmmaker's passion is a double-edged sword. Writer/directors and producers can be myopic at times. They often only see that this film absolutely, positively must be made. They believe with their whole heart that this film will make them a millionaire, or stir hearts around the world, or arouse support for a cause, or spur a distributor to sell it in all foreign territories, or inspire a studio to hire them for a 3-picture deal.

Unfortunately, many potential donors and investors do not feel the same way. Most do not believe a film will make any of these dreams a reality. Thus, without other financing options, producers enter the debt world.

When considering debt, filmmakers should consider the advantages and disadvantages of borrowing funds. Obvious advantages include:
- Debt may be the only way to finance the film and bring it to fruition.
- If the film is even a mild hit, it should generate revenues to repay the loan and interest.
- The film could generate profits for the producers above the cost of the loan.
- Loans build credibility with lenders.
- When financiers are repaid timely, they are more apt to finance the producer's next film.

Disadvantages to consider are:
- Borrowed funds must be repaid with interest.
- Penalties may accrue if payments are not made in a timely manner.
- The lender virtually always requires personal guarantees from the film owners, and possibly collateral like real estate, savings, stocks, bonds, or more.

- It may be impossible to refinance the existing loan without more collateral.
- Film seizure upon default is a risk.

If producers and filmmakers consider the risks and rewards of borrowing funds to make a film and are ready to proceed, consider Ways 39-45 using debt to finance films.

Many people first think of banks or other lenders when they hear the phrase, "film financing." But types of film financing in addition to debt include equity, non-equity donations, and soft money tax credits and incentives. Typically, film financing involves combining two or more of these methods.

The concepts of "debt" and "equity" are as different as night and day. Debt is borrowed money that must be repaid with interest within a certain timeframe, after which penalties usually apply.

Equity is an ownership interest in a production company or a film where the investment is not required to be repaid unless the film makes money. Then, equity owners are repaid for their investment plus a return before producers and back-end participants share in the profits.

Debt financing for films can be multi-layered. The first level of debt to be repaid is "senior debt" often made by banks or other entertainment lenders. Typical collateral for such debt is the film negative and domestic box office receipts.

The next level is mezzanine debt, or loans at the "mezzanine" or middle level after senior debt. The next level is gap debt covering the "gap" in the budget between the total amount needed and the amount loaned or committed.

Entertainment banks are common senior debt lenders on mid-budget and high-budget independent films, but they are not the only lending source. Hedge funds, private lending groups, financing consortiums and wealthy individuals are also sources of debt for films.

If the production company partially defaults on the loan and repays only senior debt holders, the other lenders must look for repayment from the sale of the collateral cover their loans.

If the borrower is an entity such as a limited liability company or a corporation and if no fraudulent activity or false information has been provided, the lenders are limited to selling company assets to cover their loans. The unpaid lenders could seize or sell the film, foreign sales revenues, distribution contracts and other assets until the loan is repaid in full.

Another type of film financing is slate financing in which investors finance a group, or slate, of films to diversify their risk. Slate financing is typically a joint venture between a lender or investment group and a studio or mini-major production company who agree to co-finance multiple pictures and share profits.

If a film loan is cross-collateralized with the production company's film library and the production company does not repay the loan, the lender can seize and sell enough of the library to repay the debt. Some slate financing deals have ended up in court with claims of fraudulent business practices against the studio or production company.

Another type of film financing is equity ownership where investors purchase equity interests in a film. Such sales of film equity ownerships are securities transactions subject to federal and state securities laws. Though the market fluctuates, many sources of film equity investment exist, primarily private investors. Methods of raising equity from these investors are Ways 47-50.

Banks and other entertainment lenders who provide senior debt are usually the first to be repaid. This is discussed below in Way 39.

Way 39: Banks / Senior Debt

When you think of "film financing" or "debt," a bank generally comes to mind as the lender. To obtain a loan from a senior debt financier, the producer must give a security interest in the actual film negative as well as an assignment of potential revenue streams that may be realized from its exploitation.

Producers can sell film distribution rights to domestic and foreign territories, as well as rights for television, airlines, cruise ships, military bases, online streaming, Digital Video Discs ("DVD's"), Video-On-Demand ("VOD"), Pay-Per-View ("PPV"), and many others. But lenders may require producers to assign these contracts and any resulting revenues to repay their own loans before paying other financiers. If a production company has other assets, such as an existing film library, the lender may demand the revenues from those films as additional collateral to repay the loan.

Producers typically do not pledge foreign sales revenues to senior lenders so these funds are available as collateral to junior debt lenders.

Senior debt holders are in the primary lending position. That means they hold the collateral and are the first lender to receive repayment of their interest and principal. If a producer fails to repay the loan, senior debt holders can sell the collateral to repay themselves first.

Lenders in inferior repayment positions, such as mezzanine, gap or super-gap lenders, discussed later in this Chapter, will not benefit from the sale of the collateral unless the revenues exceed the senior debt unpaid balance. At that point, the remaining proceeds are used to repay debt per the "waterfall" structure before investors, producers and back-end participants reap their reward, if any. See Chapter 19 for an explanation of the waterfall.

In the past, many banks funded production loans. However, in today's economy, some of those banks have gotten out of the film financing business. Still, a number of banks may be willing to finance films based on collateral and numerous other conditions.

Some of the most important criteria considered by banks before making a production loan are generally as follows:
- The reputation and experience of the producer;
- The collateral offered to secure the loan;
- The creditworthiness of the borrower; and
- The borrower's history and cash accounts with the bank making the loan.

Suppose this is the first film for an independent producer. She should prepare a loan package proving that she has excellent credit, a strong credit score and assets (besides the screenplay) to pledge as collateral against the loan. She should also provide proof of her equity and complete details on the film, writer, director, cast, distributor and pre-sales, if any.

If the banker personally knows the producer who has "compensating balances" of other cash accounts at the bank and opens the production account with the bank, the banker may agree to loan a percentage of the collateral pledged. This presumes the collateral can be liquidated quickly for the loan if unpaid. Such collateral includes stocks, bonds, certificates of deposit, savings and money market accounts and cash.

The next levels of debt are mezzanine, gap and super-gap, discussed below in Way 40.

Way 40: Mezzanine, Gap, Super-Gap

A film financier that makes a loan after a primary bank is a "mezzanine" lender. The loan made is for the mezzanine, which is the debt level after the senior bank loan but before other gap loans and equity.

Other collateral such as film pre-sales in foreign territories is often pledged to this level of debt. When the film begins to generate revenues and the senior debt has been fully repaid, the mezzanine lender is next to receive payment of its interest first, followed by repayment of the principal.

Even after a mezzanine lender makes a loan, there may still be a shortfall to finance the film. This amount, called the "gap," is covered by gap or super-gap lenders. They loan money to cover the difference between the total budget of a production and the financing already raised, borrowed or committed.

These loans bridge the gap in a budget between how much funding a producer has and what she needs to greenlight the film. They are typically secured by the film's foreign rights and potential future revenues from sales in any unsold foreign territories.

However, if foreign rights have been previously assigned as collateral for higher-level debt, they are not available to collateralize this loan. This would require the producer to pledge other security.

Way 41: Wrap Lenders

Lenders willing to provide a single loan that encompasses the existing loan commitments to the film are called "wrap lenders." They wrap other loans, such as conventional gap financing, discounted presales, tax credit advances, and even bridge loans, around the mezzanine loan. This financing mitigates mezzanine risk and fills the debt gap so the producer obtains his total budget.

Wrap lenders take responsibility for the underlying debt but charge interest on the total loan at a rate higher than senior debt. They make a profit on the spread between the underlying loan interest rate and the wrap rate.

Way 42: P&A Financing

After a film is produced and in post-production, a crucial step is obtaining funding for Prints and Advertising ("P&A"). This includes trailers, print ads, Electronic Press Kits ("EPK's"), TV and radio commercials, personal appearance tours, posters and other forms of promotion. This also requires release prints and other media for film festivals, exhibitors, distributors, and other screenings.

Producers must advertise the film and deliver release prints and deliverables to buyers, distributors and theaters to generate revenues. Fortunately for producers, private lenders exist that fund only P&A, though they often charge significantly higher interest rates than other lenders.

Many producers wing this part of filmmaking and dream of selling the film to a future buyer or distributor (that may or may not materialize) that will cover P&A. Others use wishful thinking in believing a festival screening or award will result in a buyer that will undertake all costs to promote the film. However, savvy producers know every film budget should include P&A, although indie films need a much smaller amount than larger ones. In today's market, it is common for P&A costs to exceed a major film's budget.

Generally, a P&A loan is made to produced films with distribution deals. P&A loans are generally not secured except with first box-office receipts, since distribution contracts, the film negative, foreign sales receipts and unsold territories are usually pledged to other lenders. Funds for P&A are released about three months before the film's theatrical release.

P&A lenders generally make these short-term loans at interest rates in the 15% to 25% range. Sometimes the lender demands a perpetual percentage of box-office revenues.

To protect their loan repayment, P&A lenders are repaid in first position after the distributor from the revenue stream. This means their loans are repaid even before secured senior debt holders. This reduces some risk of repayment for a P&A lender, although the higher interest rates compensate for the remaining risk and rarity of P&A loans.

After repaying the P&A lender and other loans, plus investors if required, any remaining profits are shared between producers and others with a back-end participation.

P&A lenders have stringent criteria, of course. However, once a P&A loan is obtained, the film can reach a greater market, can be screened and seen by distributors and film buyers and can be promoted at film markets with the funds. The producer can pay for the prints needed for film festivals, distributors, four-wall theatrical deals, and independent screenings. Film distribution is discussed in greater detail in Chapter 20.

Way 43, below, discusses slate financing, often used in multi-film projects.

Way 43: Slate Financing

One common method of film financing used primarily by large production companies and mini-major studios is slate financing, which is Way 43.

In this funding arrangement a lender, hedge fund, or other investment group funds one loan covering multiple films by the producing entity that also often distributes the pictures.

The lender cross-collateralizes all the films on the slate to diversity the risk of non-payment. So, if several films lose money but one or more is a box office success, the loan is repaid by the profitable film or films.

The slate must be approved by the lender and might include a potential blockbuster, a sequel to a popular film and several mid-level budget films. The films can also be a mix of drama, comedy, rom-com and horror films.

In slate financing deals, the studio is usually allowed to receive a lower distribution fee than usual and reimbursement of certain of its marketing or other expenses before the lender receives a return of, and a return on, its capital.

Just as with other types of debt, a slate financing fund could take a senior debt position or make a mezzanine loan, depending on the terms. Investment groups and angel networks often also participate in equity ownership of films. Equity is discussed in greater detail in Chapter 18 of this book.

Although slate financing is typically issued for a package of films with budgets totaling hundreds of millions of dollars, there is a growing trend for independent filmmakers to attempt fundraising for multi-picture slates. An indie slate hedges the risk of a single film to be able to attract lenders.

For example, a filmmaker could open a production company to produce five low-budget horror films, or three romantic comedies, or a film and a sequel adapted from a book. As long as lenders' criteria can be met in such a vehicle, indie producers can use low-budget slate financing to their advantage.

The next method of raising film financing is usually overlooked by producers -- a bank line of credit. This is Way 44, explained below.

Way 44: Line of Credit

Another source of film financing is a line of credit, Way 44. While such a credit line is generally established by a lending institution such as a bank or credit union, it is not the same as a loan.

Producers have an excellent opportunity to borrow money and repay it at their own speed with a line of credit from a bank. And, more importantly, a line of credit may be less costly than a bank loan. This is because the producer only pays interest on the amount drawn down, or borrowed, from the line until it is repaid.

To obtain a line of credit, the producer must first have good credit and a credit score acceptable to the bank. While many people think credit and credit scores are a mystery, they can be simplified in this way:

- Open and hold open a combination of revolving accounts (like credit cards, department store cards or fuel cards) and installment loans (like car loans, student loans, and mortgages);
- Pay all bills on time;
- Make at least the minimum payment every month on every debt; and
- On a monthly basis, use no more than about 60%-65%, rather than 100%, of your available credit from all sources.

Credit scores are comprised of a combination of factors, with the percentage of the total score generally computed as follows:

- History of timely payments: 35%;
- Combination of credit types: 10%;
- Use of the total credit limit: 30%;
- Length of credit use: 15%; and

- Inquiries for new credit: 10%.

If a producer borrows $10,000.00 via a loan, she receives the entire amount up front and interest starts to accumulate whether the funds are immediately used or not. At the end of the loan period, all the interest and principal are due, plus loan origination fees or bank fees charged to make the loan.

In contrast, when a bank opens a $10,000.00 line of credit for a producer, legal documents are signed for a revolving loan of up to that amount. The producer may borrow funds against the total authorized amount, then repay some and re-borrow funds as needed. Credit line interest is only owed on the amount borrowed from the time it is drawn down until it is repaid. And interest due on money borrowed may be accrued without repayment, up to the limit of the line.

Usually a bank charges a small fee to open a line of credit, then an annual fee to renew the line. This is a ready source of funds to use, pay back in whole or in part, and borrow again up to the limit.

Most financial institutions require a monthly minimum payment on a line of credit, first applied to accrued interest then to the principal amount borrowed. However, the total amount borrowed may carry forward so long as the minimum payment is made.

A line of credit is similar to a credit card, though interest generally accrues on the line's unpaid balance at a lower rate than a card.

Whether a producer draws down on her approved line for $5,000 or $500,000, she only pays interest on the draw-down for as long as it is borrowed. If she repays 80% of the amount borrowed after two months, her interest is only accrued for two months. She can continue to borrow up to the credit line limit at any time.

With a line of credit, a producer can limit the amount of interest payable, particularly if draw-downs occur late in production or post. Principal repayment of the loan can be in whole or in part unless terms state otherwise.

A producer or production company with good credit generally can obtain a line of credit without assigning film assets as collateral. However, banks often require borrowers to pledge their personal guarantee of repayment for their production company's line of credit.

A producer should be confident that the production company can repay the amount borrowed plus interest or she will be held responsible under her guarantee to pay it.

The next method of film financing is Way 45, loans advanced against tax credits.

Way 45: Tax Credit Advances

Tax credits offered by many states and foreign countries are a source of free money. However, many indie producers do not take advantage of this exceptional Way to fund a film. Way 45 is a loan collateralized with the film's future tax credits.

This section focuses on loans against domestic tax credits offered by U.S. states, while Way 46 discusses foreign jurisdiction incentives and production rebate schemes.

As discussed in Way 36, production companies often sell their film tax credits to individual or corporate taxpayers in the state in which the credits were earned. At other times, producers sell at a deep discount to brokers who re-sell the credits to taxpayers and keep a hefty spread. But both types of sales only generate funds after the picture is produced and all the expenses have been paid.

For a producer who is short of making her budget, a common financing alternative before commencing principal photography is a tax credit loan. Brokers and other lenders loan against future tax credits to be earned. As actual production expenditures often differ from the budget, the final advance may be reduced by one or more factors, such as:

- The risk that the production may not be approved for all anticipated credits;
- Prepaid interest on the loan;
- The broker's profit margin, or spread; and
- A holdback to cover additional months of interest if the production incurs delays.

When the picture is completed and the production expenditures have been audited if necessary and approved, the tax credit lender retains the tax credits that cover his loan, interest, and profit spread.

In some cases, tax credit brokers keep all the credits, even if they exceed all of the loan costs. The brokers are able to sell the credits for a large spread, increasing their profit above their loan principal and interest. Producers should try to mitigate risk for such lenders so the producers obtain the largest advance possible.

Way 46: Foreign Incentives

Many foreign countries and regions located around the world offer incentives to attract productions to those locations. Way 46 is using foreign incentives to fund part of the budget.

Some international jurisdictions offer tax credits or rebates on a film's local production expenditures. Complex application documents and supporting financial information must be submitted to the authority before commencing production. Rebates or credits, as the case may be, are issued many months later in the currency of the jurisdiction. Producers must absorb the risk of currency value and exchange rates over which they have no control.

Other foreign locations offer a variety of different incentives ranging from discounts on goods and services to free services. Some are members of AFCI as discussed earlier. All foreign jurisdictions should be researched for the best incentives possible for a producer.

Ways 47 through 50 discuss how to raise film financing through the sales of film ownership interests, which are referred to as equity securities.

18.

EQUITY SECURITIES
Ways 47-50 of 50

Raising film financing from private investors can be confusing to producers. An attorney with expertise in securities law and entertainment law, if possible, should be consulted before offering or selling any ownership equity in a film or production company.

Why? Because these equity interests are "securities" subject to U.S. securities laws and regulated by the Securities and Exchange Commission ("SEC"). The federal Securities Act of 1933 ("1933 Act") requires security offers and sales to be registered with the SEC or to qualify for a registration exemption.

Registration of these "public offerings" is very expensive and time-consuming and requires continued regular SEC filings.

However, producers can access registration exemptions to offer and sell equity securities in a film or its production company through a "private placement" or "private offering." The producer can legally raise film financing from private investors by relying on a registration exemption, including Ways 47 through 50. Way 47 which follows is the SEC Regulation Crowdfunding private placement.

Way 47: SEC Regulation Crowdfunding

Way 47, SEC Regulation Crowdfunding, should not be confused with online donor crowdfunding sites. These sites are the ones that collect donations but do not offer and sell equity interests in companies and films.

In contrast, Regulation Crowdfunding online portals are legally allowed to accept investors' funds to buy equity interests in companies that include film production companies. These ownership interests are equity securities that require registration with the SEC or an exemption from registration.

In 2015, Congress enacted into federal law, Title III of the Jumpstart Our Business Startups Act ("JOBS") of 2012. It includes the Securities Act Section 4(a)(6). This legislation provides the Regulation Crowdfunding exemption from SEC registration. Now, producers can raise film financing by legally selling ownership equity interests in their film or production company.

Producers can utilize this SEC Regulation Crowdfunding exemption by first setting up a production company. The company is the entity that raises investment capital for a film.

This company owns the film and is the "issuer" that offers and sells the security interests in the film. It can be a limited liability company, corporation or other legal entity.

For a film, the securities are the ownership equity interests in the issuer company. The owners are the initial founders of the issuing company as well as the investors who meet the requirements of this exemption.

Investors can only participate in this SEC Regulation Crowdfunding offering by using a registered online platform of an intermediary. Intermediaries include registered securities broker-dealers and funding portals. These broker-dealers must be registered with the SEC and be a member of FINRA, the Financial Industry Regulatory Authority. Also, funding portals must be registered with the SEC and abide by its governing rules.

To qualify for the Regulation Crowdfunding exemption from SEC registration, the issuer producers must use an intermediary to offer ownership securities. Issuers are not allowed to make direct contact to offer or sell their film interests to potential buyers. Bypassing the intermediary to communicate directly with an investor could be considered an offer and/or advertising of securities. These actions violate federal law and require SEC registration or another exemption for such an offering.

Producers are able to utilize Regulation Crowdfunding as a legal method to raise film financing. This exemption allows them to offer and sell equity interests in the production company of film to private investors.

To be able to rely on this exemption, certain requirements must be met, as described below.

1. Maximum Offering of $1,070,000

The SEC has set the maximum offering amount that an issuer, i.e., the company offering its securities, may raise in reliance on a Regulation Crowdfunding exemption from SEC registration.

In a 12-month period, that amount was one million dollars and is now $1,070,000. The maximum investment limit by a single investor in an offering is now $107,000. The maximum amount of securities that an issuer can sell in a single offering includes:

- The amount it has already sold relying on Regulation Crowdfunding during the 12-month period preceding the expected date of sale; this includes amounts sold by entities controlled by, or under common control with, the issuer, and any amounts sold by any predecessor of the issuer; *plus*,
- The amount the issuer intends to raise in this offering while relying on the Regulation Crowdfunding exemption.

An issuer relying on any securities exemptions in the 12 months prior to the current offering date other than Regulation Crowdfunding does not aggregate the above amounts into the current offering total.

2. Investor Limits

Another requirement of SEC Regulation Crowdfunding is the amounts individual investors can legally invest in multiple Regulation Crowdfunding offerings over the 12-month period are limited.

Investors must meet a two-prong test to determine the maximum amount they can invest in a particular offering -- net worth and income. The net worth test is the investor's total assets minus total liabilities, subject to certain restrictions. A minimum income is required, subject to limitations.

The fair market value of the investor's primary residence is excluded from assets. A mortgage, home equity line or other loan on the primary residence is not deducted as a liability, up to the fair market value of the home. If an investor's home is "under water" and the homeowner owes more on the house than its fair market value, any loan amount above this value is a liability that is deducted from other assets.

The limits relate to an investor's annual income and net worth for the purpose of a single investment. The value of his primary residence and the mortgage up to that value is excluded from net worth. Spouses may calculate annual income and net worth jointly, *excluding* the value of their primary residence and the mortgage up to that value,

An investor is subject to three limitation tests, as described below:
- If *either* an investor's annual income *or* his net worth is less than $107,000, then his investment limit is the greater of:
    - $2,200; or
    - 5 percent (5%) of the *lesser* of the investor's annual income *or* net worth.
- If *both* an investor's annual income *and* net worth are equal to or more than $107,000, the investor's limit is:
    - 10 percent (10%) of the *lesser* of their annual income or net worth.
- During the current 12-month period, the aggregate amount of securities sold to an investor in *all* Regulation Crowdfunding offerings in which he invests may not exceed $107,000, *regardless of the investor's annual income or net worth.*

What happens if a producer meets a potential buyer who previously invested the legal limit in any other SEC Regulation Crowdfunding offering? Unfortunately for the current offering issuer, the investor is prohibited from investing in it until that investor's 12-month period expires.

Chart 18 which follows illustrates several examples of specific limits on an investor based on his annual income, net worth, or both. His maximum investment total in the period, referred to as the "Cap," is $107,000, regardless of annual income or net worth.

TABLE 18
Equity Investment Limits Based on Annual Income or Net Worth, Subject to Maximum Investment Caps

Annual Income	Net Worth (subject to exclusions)	Formula to Calculate	Investment Limit
$150,000	$80,000	Greater of $2,200 or 5% of $80,000	$4,000
$150,000	$107,000	10% of $107,000	$10,700
$200,000	$900,000	10% of $200,000	$20,000
$1,200,000	$2,000,000	Lower of 10% of $1,200,000 or Cap	$107,000 Maximum Investment Cap

3. Exclusive Intermediary for Transactions

Each offering utilizing the Regulation Crowdfunding exemption must be made exclusively through an online platform conducted by a specific intermediary.

The intermediary must be a broker-dealer or a funding portal registered with the SEC and with the Financial Industry Regulatory Authority ("FINRA"). FINRA is a self-regulating organization but is not a government agency.

Funding portal information is available on the SEC EDGAR site at www. sec.gov/edgar/searchedgar/companysearch.html.

Investors and issuers can research specific broker-dealers on the FINRA BrokerCheck link at www.brokercheck.finra.

org, or by calling its toll-free BrokerCheck hotline on 1.800.289.9999.

The issuer does not have any knowledge if the investor's purchase in the current offering would cause the investor to exceed the legal investment limits. The one who determines an investor's aggregate amount of purchased securities is the intermediary. An issuer may rely on this determination as to whether the investor may buy an equity interest in the offering.

4. Issuer Disclosures

A production company or producer who is the issuer of an offering must file its offering statement electronically pursuant to Regulation Crowdfunding. The statement is filed on Form C on the SEC's Electronic Data Gathering, Analysis and Retrieval system ("EDGAR") and is also filed with the intermediary facilitating the crowdfunding equity offering.

Form C requires substantial disclosures about the issuer and the offering, including, but not limited to the following:
- A description of the issuer's business and the offering's use of proceeds;
- Information about officers, directors, and owners of twenty percent or more of the issuer;
- The issuer's financial condition and statements;

FINANCING INDEPENDENT FILMS | 171

- The targeted amount of the offering and the expected deadline to reach it;
- If investments exceeding the target offering will be accepted;
- Certain transactions between related parties; and
- The securities price to the public, or the method to determine such price if the price is unknown.

5. Financial Statement Requirements

Requirements for financial statements of issuers are based on the amount offered and sold in a Regulation Crowdfunding offering within the immediately preceding 12-month period.

An independent accountant must review or audit all of the issuer's financial statements at certain issue dollar levels. Accountant independence refers to one who is not regularly engaged in the issuing company's accounting or auditing functions. Some restrictions are described below.

If an issuer offers securities of $107,000 or less, the issuer must provide financial statements and specific federal income tax information certified by the principal executive officer of the issuer, unless financial statements are available after audit or review by an independent accountant or auditor.

For any securities offering greater than $107,000 but not more than $535,000, the

issuer must provide financial statements reviewed by an independent accountant, or financials audited by an independent auditor, if available. For securities offerings greater than $535,000, issuers must provide:
- Financial statements reviewed by an independent public accountant or, if available, financials audited by an independent auditor when offered by a first-time Regulation Crowdfunder; or
- Financial statements audited by a public accountant independent of the issuer, if offered by an issuer that previously relied on Regulation Crowdfunding in another offering.

6. Reporting Requirements

Issuers are required to file offering Progress Reports on Form C-U within 5 business days after obtaining sales of 50% and 100% of the target offering amount, and if the issuer accepts proceeds over the target amount.

If the intermediary files updates on its platform, the issuer may only need to file the final Form C-U with the total amount of securities sold in the offering. Issuers are also required to file Annual Reports on Form C-AR within 120 days after the end of an issuer's fiscal year, and every year thereafter.

One exception is a "termination event." This is a situation in which the issuer:
- Has fewer than 300 record holders of the securities;
- Has filed at least three annual reports and has assets of $10 million or less; or
- Has liquidated and is dissolved under state law.

If legal liquidation or dissolution occurs, the issuer must file notice on Form C-TR that it will no longer file annual reports for Regulation Crowdfunding. Other reporting requirements may also be required.

7. Eligibility

To use the Regulation Crowdfunding exemption, companies must be eligible. Certain companies that are ineligible to use this exemption include those that are:
- Not U.S. companies;
- Certain investment companies;
- Companies disqualified by the rules;
- Exchange Act reporting companies;
- Companies without a specific business plan or a merger and acquisition plan with an unidentified company;
- Companies that have not complied with the Regulation Crowdfunding annual reporting requirements during the two years before filing the offering statement; and
- Other exclusions.

8. Advertising and Promoter Limitations

In an SEC Regulation Crowdfunding offering, an issuer may not advertise except in a notice that directs investors to the intermediary's platform. The notice can only include specific information about:
- The Reliance Statement of the issuer pursuant to Section 4(a)(6) of the Securities Act;
- The nature, price and terms of the offering and the securities offered;
- Information about the issuer's legal identity, business location and contact information; and
- The name and a link to the platform of the intermediary.

The issuer may communicate the terms of the offering with potential investors only if it uses the intermediary's communication channels on its platform and identifies itself as the issuer.

Any person acting for the issuer must identity his affiliation with the issuer in all such communications.

A person who is a "promoter" of a Regulation Crowdfunding offering on an intermediary's communications channels can receive compensation from an issuer.

However, the issuer must be diligent in assuring that the promoter payments are disclosed in each communication about such offering.

9. Restrictions on Resale

One of the restrictions on the securities purchased in a Regulation Crowdfunding offering is a restriction on resales for a certain period, usually one year. However, certain exceptions apply, including if the purchaser sells the securities:
- To the issuer;
- To an "accredited investor;"
- As part of an offering that is registered with the SEC; or
- To certain family members or trusts, or upon divorce, death or other such major events.

10. Bad Actor Disqualification

Rule 503 of Regulation Crowdfunding includes criteria that disqualify offerings if the issuer or other "covered persons" are "bad actors" who have experienced a disqualifying event.

Such events include certain criminal convictions, court injunctions, restraining orders, SEC disciplinary orders, and other final state or federal regulatory orders. Certain such events occurring before May 16, 2016 that would otherwise be considered disqualifying are exempt but they must still be disclosed in the offering statement.

Covered persons include the issuer and its directors, officers, general partners or managing members, as well as promoters connected with the issuer at time of sale, beneficial owners of twenty percent or more of the issuer's outstanding voting equity securities, and any persons receiving compensation for soliciting investors.

Another exemption from SEC securities registration is the "California Exemption." This is applicable to certain production companies locating or operating in California or with the majority of its property, payroll or owners in California. More details on this Way 48 follow.

Way 48: California Exemption

In addition to Regulation Crowdfunding, a valuable exemption to securities registration by film owners is SEC Rule 1001. This is Way 48, referred to as the "California Exemption."

This exemption is generally limited to securities issuers that fit one of two categories:
- A California corporation or another business entity organized in the state; or
- A non-California organized business that:
  - Attributes more than fifty percent of its property, payroll and sales to California; and
  - Has over fifty percent of the outstanding voting securities of the issuing company held by persons with California addresses.

This exemption can be used for any businesses that meet the above requirements. In film financing, the exemption is important for California production companies since it allows general, but limited, solicitation of investors. Most other types of exemptions from securities registration do not allow *any* type of solicitation.

California production companies can use this exemption to raise capital to finance their operations, projects and growth for one film or a slate of pictures.

Using this exemption, a qualified California production company can raise financing by selling equity in its films if certain criteria are met, including that:

- The company offers and sells no more than $5 million of securities in one offering in a 12-month period;
- All offers are made only to a "qualified purchaser," defined as:
  - A natural person whose net worth exceeds $500,000, or a natural person whose net worth exceeds $250,000 if his annual income exceeds $100,000;
  - Certain relatives residing with a qualified person;
  - Any person purchasing more than $150,000 of securities in the offering;
  - The issuer's directors or affiliates; and
  - Other requirements.
- General solicitation of offerees is limited;
- Securities issued under this exemption are "restricted securities" that can only be resold by registering the securities or reliance on another exemption;

- A notice is filed with the California Corporations Commission that includes certain disclosures, fees and subsequent filing(s); and
- Other requirements.

Even with the complexities of securities laws and regulations, violations can result in civil or criminal fines and penalties. It is crucial that producers consult a securities attorney prior to attempting to raise any film financing through the sale of equity ownership interests in a film or production company offering.

This information is merely a summary and is not a complete list of all requirements and criteria necessary for such exemption. However, the availability of the California Exemption from registration for qualified production companies is an additional alternative for seeking film financing.

The next exemption is Way 49, for securities offered and sold within a single state.

Way 49: Intrastate Exemption 1: Section 3(a)(11)

Another exemption to securities registration for the sale of film equity interests available to producers and film owners is Section 3(a)(11) of the Securities Act of 1933. This is an "Intrastate Exemption" for securities that are offered and sold only within one state.

Producers selling film equity interests to raise film financing for a film in one state can take advantage of this exemption. They must comply with the qualifying restrictions of the

Section 3(a)(11) exemption that require the issuer to:
- Be a resident of, or incorporated or organized in, or have its principal office located in, the state where it offers the securities for sale;
- Carry out a significant amount of its business activities in that state; and
- Make offers and sales of securities only to residents of that state.

This exemption does not limit the number of offerees, number of purchasers, or size of the offering, nor prohibit general advertising or solicitation if in compliance with state law and offers and sales are made only to residents.

Rule 147 of the Securities Act of 1933 provides "Safe Harbor" provisions to prevent the "integration" of other offers and sales of equity interests to non-residents with those to residents in an Intrastate Offering, thus losing the exemption. Some criteria include if they:
- Are part of a single plan of financing;
- Issue the same class of securities;
- Receive the same type of consideration;
- Are made at or about the same time; and
- Are made for the same general purpose.

The issuer should verify that each offeree and purchaser is a resident of the state where the equity interests are offered. An offer or sale to one non-resident can end the Intrastate Exemption. Then the offering needs to be registered or qualified for another exemption.

Resales of exempt securities are prohibited for nine months after purchase except if made in the same state as the intrastate offering.

These are only some of the regulations related to the Intrastate Exemption. Way 50 provides another type of Intrastate Exemption, which was adopted by the SEC in 2017.

Way 50: Intrastate Exemption 2: Rule 147A

In 2017, the SEC adopted a new Intrastate Exemption, Rule 147A, as part of the Securities Act of 1933. The purpose is to assist small businesses, like film production companies, raise financing without onerous restrictions on offers and sales of equity interests in such companies. However, sales may be made only to residents of the issuer's state to maintain the intrastate nature of the exemption.

Another difference between 3(a)(11) and Rule 147A is that the latter Rule does not require an issuer, like a production company, to be incorporated or organized in the same state where the offering occurs.

Like Rule 147, the issuer in Rule 147A must still demonstrate the in-state nature of their business operations. The issuer must also fulfill other requirements, which include, but are not limited to, mandatory disclosures to offerees and buyers, and compliance with state securities laws.

*

You now have 50 Ways to raise or reduce your film budget. Review the Ways again, choose those that best suit your style, timing, objectives and budget.

It's time to go for it!

IV

MONEY, MONEY, MONEY

Where It All Goes

19.

THE WATERFALL

One of the major responsibilities of a producer in producing a film is keeping accurate, organized financial records. Proper financial accounting and record-keeping is crucial to determine if the production is under, over, or on budget and has the funds to pay the bills when due.

Producers should engage an experienced production accountant during development. This accounting professional will set up the books of account and create the procedures to retain receipts and keep financial records current. If the production hires a payroll company to handle salaries, taxes, union payments and other costs, the accountant can coordinate and be a liaison for the film.

If a producer is doing a micro-budget film and cannot afford a production accountant or a payroll company, the producer can designate herself or another qualified person to do so. She should devote a period of time, preferably daily, to record purchases, rentals, deposits, returns, taxes, above-the-line and below-the-line payments and all other transactions.

Producers need to know at all times if the production is on budget and the variances, if any, from the actual budget. Inexpensive specialized computer software is available to streamline the process and to provide up-to-date reports for the production team as well as financiers and any investors. Such reports are usually required by financing agreements, but even if not, it is good business to keep lenders and investors informed of the film's finances.

By setting up proper accounting records in advance, producers exhibit the efficiency, organization and professionalism that lenders view positively. Likewise, equity owners look for and rely on film accounting records and budgets to monitor their investment, expenses and potential repayment of their investment and (hopefully) a return.

How well a producer maintains and reports financial records may also make a difference for subsequent films.

Now comes the part you've been waiting for -- producer profits. Unfortunately, they may not be realized overnight, if at all. Filmmakers and producers who conceive the project, put skin in the game, beg or borrow the rest of the financing, produce the film and exploit it by themselves or a third-party distributor will not receive a penny of profits until the waterfall of creditors is repaid.

Waterfall? What waterfall?

When referring to revenues earned by a film, the "waterfall" means the order in which everyone owed money or a back-end by the film is paid. The waterfall also specifies the priority of payments to lenders who provide production finance and P&A loans.

Lenders are the first to receive repayment of loans, with interest. Next, equity investors recoup their money and any guaranteed preferred returns. The producer is last to receive any profits, usually paid on a pari passu basis. This is payment simultaneously paid to them and back-end profit participants.

The irony of the waterfall is that the actual owners of the film who take the greatest risk are the last to receive equity return and profit.

The typical order of priority repayments in the waterfall, from the first to be repaid until the last, follows:

1. P&A lender that is the last money in, and first money out, repaying their loans to advertise the film and pay for release prints for theater screenings.
2. Senior debt holders, such as banks. Providers of senior debt traditionally require collateral to secure such loans. This could include the value of distribution contracts and, of course, the negative of the film so that the owners cannot make prints or receive film sales proceeds until these lenders are repaid.

3. Junior debt holders, such as mezzanine, gap and super-gap financiers.
4. Deferrals (unless contracts require these fees and costs to be paid prior to repaying other lenders).
5. Investor preferred return and equity repayment.
6. Investor, producer(s) and back-end participants in profit-sharing.

Once a finished film is distributed, the funds received from all sales and distribution contracts are sent to the production company, or to its assignee. A contract for loans with a bank, mezzanine lender, P&A fund, gap lender or other such financier generally includes the assignment of such revenues to repay these lenders pursuant to the waterfall.

Debts that must be repaid before the producer receives any profits include deferrals to cast and crew, professional fees, such as those for attorneys and accountants, and other outstanding production expenses.

Before the producer receives a dime from the film receipts, the investors must be repaid as well. Presuming a private offering was completed, equity investors receive a return of their investment after all debt is repaid. Then the equity investors receive a preferred return if it is a condition of the investment.

The equity investor return is considered "preferred" because the investor receives it before the producer receives her share of any funds. There is no hard and fast rule about how much this preferred return should be. It can range from five to about twenty percent or so.

After the investors are repaid their investment plus their preferred return, then the producer shares the profit with the investors. The most common split is 50/50, which means 50% is paid to investors after they receive the return of their investment and preferred return, and 50% to the production company as the producer's share.

Some parties receive back-end percentage participations, such as the lead talent, writer, director and others if such a sweetener is needed to attach them or to obtain deferrals of their compensation. These profit shares are paid at the same time as the producer out of the "producer's share" as opposed to the "investor's share." Back-end profits are not guaranteed so they are not a producer liability.

The profit split terms are not set by law but are subject to negotiation between the producer and the investors. A negotiable term is whether the return is a preferred or a cumulative one, or both.

Preferred returns are paid to investors prior to paying the producer's share. Cumulative returns carry over from year to year until paid before the producer's share. If revenues are too low to pay investors, the producer might wait years for any return on her skin in the game, creative effort and sweat equity in the film.

As described above, not all production company profit split goes to the producer or filmmaker who spearheaded the project and made it happen.

Consider the following hypothetical of the waterfall to recoup loans and investment.

A producer needs $900,000 to make her film budget of $1 million, after she has invested $100,000 of her own cash. The film's talent and producers defer partial compensation of $100,000. A bank loans $450,000 at 8% interest and a gap lender loans $200,000 at 15% annual interest. Using the CA Intrastate Exemption (see Chapter 18), the producer sells equity in the film to in-state investors for $150,000. The equity investors receive the full 100% of their investment and a preferred non-cumulative return of 5%, then a 50% share on a "pari passu" basis with the producer; i.e., paid at the same time. The producer's 50% is reduced to 30% with the remaining 20% paid as a 5% backend to each of the writer, principal actor, director and executive producer. The producer has not arranged for a P&A loan but anticipates a potential sale when the film premieres at a festival. At the sale, one year's interest is due.

Table 19 displays the waterfall recoupment schedule to repay $650,000 of debt, $100,000 of deferrals and $150,000 of equity investment on a film budget of $1 million. Three different amounts of total receipts of a film (after exhibitor and distributor fees, if any) are projected at $800,000, $1 million and $2 million. Principal and interest on each loan is shown, as well as deferral payments, equity investor repayment, back-end participation and the producer's profit, if any.

TABLE 19
Waterfall at 3 Levels of Film Receipts: $800,000; $1 Million; $2 Million

Type of Payment	$800,000	$1 Million	$2 Million
Senior Loan Interest	$36,000	$36,000	$36,000
Senior Loan Principal	$450,000	$450,000	$450,000
Gap Loan Interest	$30,000	$30,000	$30,000
Gap Loan Principal	$200,000	$200,000	$200,000
Deferrals Paid	$84,000	$100,000	$100,000
Balance Available	**$0**	**$184,000**	**$1,184,000**
Unpaid Deferrals	$16,000	$0	$0
Equity Preferred Return	$0	$7,500	$7,500
Equity Principal Paid	$0	$150,000	$150,000
Unpaid Equity & Return	$165,000	-	-
Balance Available	**$0**	**$26,500**	**$1,026,500**
Investor Share (50%)	$0	$13,250	$513,250
Back-end Director, Writer, EP, Star (20%)	$0 Ea. $0	$5,300 Ea.$1,325	$205,300 Ea. $51,325
Producer Share (30%) (50% reduced by 20% backend participations above)	$0	$7,950 ($92,050 less than $100,000 paid in)	$307,950 ($207,950 more than $100,000 paid in)

V

DISTRIBUTION & BEYOND

Get Your Film Out There

20.

DISTRIBUTION

Even before a film is produced, the producer should decide how she will sell the film. A strong exploitation plan is crucial to generating revenues for a film. The different types of distribution are discussed hereafter.

A. DOMESTIC DISTRIBUTION

Distribution can take many forms including:
- Theatrical release;
- Free television;
- Basic cable television;
- Premium cable television;
- Home video/DVD/Blu-ray;
- VOD/PPV (Video-On-Demand/Pay-Per-View); and
- Digital/Online.

As discussed in Chapter 7, Producer's Reps and Foreign Sales Agents are optional elements of the distribution process, assisting producers to market their films domestically and internationally.

The following discussions describe film distribution methods used by third parties and producers.

1. Theatrical Distribution

Theatrical distribution is the king of all distribution methods. However, it has the unfortunate reputation of being the most difficult to obtain. This is true even though films are theatrically released in many ways.

Independent filmmakers may have the opportunity to exploit their films using one or more of these methods, depending on whether they have a distribution deal or if they are self-distributing the film.

These types of distribution include:

- *Major (Wide) Theatrical Release*: This is the method of distributing films in thousands of theaters across the country. Wide distribution of movies is primarily reserved for studio and mini-major studio films, or award-winning movies in which substantial P&A funds are invested to promote the films and generate box office revenues. Distributors usually pay all P&A costs. The producer is paid based on the deal or at the film sale.
- *Limited Theatrical Release*: This type of distribution consists of releasing a film in a few hundred theaters or

more across the country. Sometimes the film is released only in a few large cities like New York and Los Angeles. Limited film releases are generally done by studios that also distribute films they buy at major film festivals.

- *Four-Wall or Percentage Deal*: This type of distribution is a do-it-yourselfer. The producer rents the "four walls" of a theater for a week in advance, then retains the box office receipts of the showings. Sometimes a theater owner may accept a percentage of box office sales rather than a fixed rental price up front. Such a Four-Wall agreement is risky for the producer because she is out the rental fee if she does not sell enough tickets to cover it. The Percentage Deal is risky for the theater owner who must believe the producer can fill enough seats for the theater to profit during that period.

- *One-Night Only or Limited Engagement Screenings*: In this deal, the producer holds screenings of the film on one or more nights in different cities across the country using a screening events company. This method costs the producer substantial time and money. It is her responsibility to attract audiences in each city by promoting the film in advance of the night or nights that the movie is playing there.

- *Service Deal Theatrical Release*: This distribution method is one in which the producer signs a contract with a theatrical distributor, generally for a negotiated fee lower than usual and a percentage of the film's box office receipts. This is often called a "rent-a-distributor" deal in which the film is released into theaters and in which the distributor also generally acts as the press liaison. The producer gets a break on the distribution fee but is responsible for paying all the P&A costs.

2. DVD/Blu-ray, VOD, PPV (Home Video, Video-On-Demand and Pay-Per-View)

    Home video sales and rentals of indie films on DVD and Blu-ray have the potential to generate substantially more than total theatrical box office revenues. These opportunities are described below.
    - *DVD and Blu-ray Sales and Rentals*: While physical locations that sell and rent films on DVD and Blu-ray are decreasing, demand for the products is not slowing down. Producers can list films online in many internet stores selling physical discs and can also include the films in catalogues of dozens of home video distributors.
    - *Video-On-Demand or Pay-Per-View*: Filmmakers generally have little to no

experience in working with different platforms for VOD or PPV. However, a number of options are available to license films with internet, satellite, cable, telecommunications and other such providers. Some companies ask for a substantial fee up front, but it is sometimes possible to obtain a short-term arrangement for several months on a split revenue system without a hefty advance payment. Producers do not need a lawyer to negotiate these deals, although specialist distributors offer these services for a fee. The key to fiscal success in the VOD market is to make sure buyers know where to find your film, which might require buying advertising on the platform(s) where the film is. In this case, it may be better to invest in ads for the chance to reap a larger reward in sales than to pay a distributor *plus* pay for ad buys at the filmmaker's cost.

B. DISTRIBUTION DEAL STRUCTURES

Four common deal structures are used to acquire and/or distribute independent films.

1. Production & Distribution

In a Production & Distribution deal, an outside production company or studio acquires the project from the producer or filmmaker, finances the movie and self-distributes it.

The production company or studio will negotiate with the producer on terms like back-end, compensation and screen credit. However, the person who brought the project to the new production company usually has no control over the production.

All decision-making concerning the film, including, but not limited to, cast, budget, and script changes, are in the hands of the acquiring company, not the project creator. If the studio or production company keeps the creator attached, it is as a work-for-hire employee or contractor.

This is not a pre-sale since the acquiring company buys the screenplay or story idea, then develops, produces and distributes the film in-house or through an affiliate.

2. Acquisition & Distribution Deal

An Acquisition & Distribution Deal is a method of financing a film in which a producer raises investor funds or borrows money to acquire a non-produced project from a third-party filmmaker who created it. The producer also raises investment monies or loans to produce and complete the film.

After completing a film, a third-party distributor covers the marketing and P&A costs. The acquiring producer has creative control over the project but also bears the risk of repaying loans and investors.

3. Domestic Distribution -- Theatrical

Theatrical domestic distribution deals are a form of financing distribution in domestic theaters once the film is already financed. The producer obtains financing to acquire any literary material rights and to develop and produce the film. The distributor covers all distribution expenses, including film markets, P&A and more.

In another version of this deal, the producer raises the financing necessary to acquire literary material and develop and package the film, attaching a director and the principal cast. The producer takes the film to a distributor or studio distribution arm that provides financing to produce and distribute it.

At distribution, the financier receives distribution expenses, fees and loan interest and principal. Box office and other receipts cover or reduce the film negative cost before the producer receives a profit share.

4. Domestic Distribution -- Non-Theatrical

Many ways exist to exploit a film domestically outside of, or in addition to, theatrical distribution. These include home video (Blu-ray and DVD), premium cable television, basic cable television, airlines, cruise ships, military, television, phone/telecommunications and internet VOD (Video on Demand).

Independent filmmakers should ask themselves how they can exploit their films to the greatest extent and on the greatest number of platforms, particularly with today's technology.

High-traffic sites such as Amazon, iTunes, Xbox and others are open to new films. But filmmakers should also self-promote their films on their production company or film websites and social media outlets.

No matter on which platforms a producer wants to distribute her film, she should be armed with all the marketing tools possible before pitching the film.

To maximize revenues, a producer must be prepared to reach the market with extraordinary elements:

- Film poster and original artwork to which the producer owns all of the copyrights (either through her own creativity or by hiring graphic artists on work-for-hire contracts);
- Strong social media marketing;
- Maintaining existing followers and building a new fan base;
- Press coverage, releases and public relations favorable to the film;
- Viral (hopefully) videos; and
- Other available promotional tools.

After a film is accepted by online sites, the producer should continue to work and advertise to drive as much traffic to her film on the site. By doing so, she can create greater buzz and generate greater revenues.

5. Negative Pick-Up

A negative pick-up is another form of film financing although it is not often applied to independent film producers. This method is considered production-money financing. The producer obtains sufficient financing to produce the film and procures pre-sale guarantees from distributors to buy the film once it is completed. The price, delivery terms and markets which are being purchased are fixed in this commitment.

The producer can use this distribution commitment as collateral to borrow the production financing needed to complete the film. The distributor can provide P&A funds for distributing the film which will be purchased upon completion.

6. Rent-a-Distributor / Rent-a-Studio

This is a form of financing in which a producer has already obtained the necessary production funding and produced her film.

The producer might still need funding for distribution so this financing method is particularly attractive to distributors. But the film should be at least a rough cut, if not in final form, before a distributor is approached.

The near-complete status of the film reduces the sales risk for a distributor. Generally, the distributor will accept a lower domestic distribution commission of about 15%, rather than the "standard" distribution fees ranging up to 30% or so.

The distributor, which may be a major studio's distribution arm, does not advance funds for the movie. This reduces the distributor's costs.

The distributor also has the opportunity to view the finished (or nearly finished) film and gauge its value in the marketplace. This lessens the distributor's risk since it has the luxury of comparing the immediate needs of domestic and international buyers with the film's star power, production quality and competition.

However, this type of distribution poses a greater risk to the producer. For example, distributors might screen the finished film and not like it enough to buy it. They may have films in their catalogue which are too similar, or have similar films that are not selling. The distributors might discover that the cast is not desirable in potential markets or that the market value does not justify their efforts, even at a lower distribution fee. In the end, they may have numerous other objections to buying the film, leaving the producer without distribution at that point.

21.

CHAIN OF TITLE & DELIVERABLES

A producer must understand the chain of title and deliverables required by buyers and distributors of a film. Sales agents usually request the chain of title to verify ownership of the rights to the film and its elements. They may not require all deliverables, depending on a particular agent's role.

In the film industry, the phrase "chain of title" refers to all of the agreements and other documents that identify and establish the ownership rights and copyrights in a film. The chain of title starts with the screenplay or the story or treatment on which the script is based.

The term "deliverables" means all of the legal documents (including a clear chain of title), print and publicity materials and the film or digital files in the formats required by a buyer or distributor of a film.

A chain of title includes documentation for all ownership rights associated with the film and its elements. These include screenplay creation and ownership, copyright registration and all transfer agreements like options, acquisitions, licenses and reversions of any of the rights to the film.

A clean chain of title is required to transfer film rights to third party buyers and licensees. Similar to selling ownership interests in real estate or vehicles, a clean film chain of title assures the buyer that he is the sole and exclusive owner of the rights he is acquiring in and to the picture.

Clearing defects in a chain of title can be time-consuming and expensive. Therefore, a clean chain of title should be maintained during the entire process from material acquisition or creation through distribution.

A motion picture chain of title can be created in any way that is acceptable to the potential buyer or licensee. Typically, a chain of title is prepared in chronological order. The document should be updated continually with each transaction affecting the ownership of the property. These transactions include any and all options, sales, licenses and reversions.

If requested by the potential buyer for due diligence, copies of the original documents that evidence the rights transactions are delivered with the chain of title. At the sale of the rights to the motion picture, the original documents are provided as part of the assignment and transfer of rights to the new owner.

One of the marks of a professional producer is an up-to-date clean chain of title. Even before the film is made, a producer may have granted an option on a screenplay. Or she may have written the script herself or paid a third party on a work-for-hire agreement to write it.

In the first instance, the producer has an exclusive option on the rights and the owner cannot sell it from under her until the option expires and the producer does not purchase the screenplay. In the latter example, the producer owns all the rights to the script.

In the above situations, a chain of title can and should be created for the screenplay prior to production of the film.

Once in production, the producer should update the chain of title as additional relevant rights documents are executed. These include copyright registrations of revised screenplays as well as the completed film. A director's cut should be copyrighted in addition to the original final film.

Update the chain of title with each new agreement so it will be current whenever a distributor or foreign sales agent asks to verify it. Since some indie film distribution deals are done prior to a film's completion, a producer can have the documentation ready by doing so.

Another reason for having a clean, current chain of title is that distributors detest cleaning up title issues. Many will pass on a film with an incomplete or erroneous title, even if it is well-made. This is because distributors must incur substantial legal fees and time to clear the title of a motion picture.

For a film clean chain of title, a partial list of documents and agreements needed includes:
- Acquisition Agreements;
- Assignments of Rights;
- Certificate of Authorship;
- Certificate of Copyright Registration;
- Clearances:
  - Film Title (name),
  - Trademarks, and
  - Screenplay (cities, brands, logos, etc.);
- Distribution Licenses & Territories;
- Film/Video Clip Licenses;
- Literary Rights Acquisition;
- Music Clearances and Licenses:
  - Composer,
  - Songwriter,
  - Synchronization,
  - Master Use, and
  - Master Recording;
- Option;
- Option and Acquisition;
- Photograph Releases;
- Property and Design Rights Agreements;
- Releases:
  - Crowd Releases,
  - Extra Releases,
  - Minor Releases, and
  - Location Releases;
- Reversionary Rights Agreements;
- Screenplay;
- Talent Loanout Agreements;
- Treatment;
- Work-for-Hire Agreements.

- Writer,
- Director,
- Producer,
- Writer/Director,
- Cinematographer,
- Set Designer,
- Costume Designer,
- Artist,
- Graphic Designer,
- Property Designer,
- Composer, and
- Photographer;
* And other documents affecting rights ownership of a film and its elements.

The Forms Bank in the back of this book provides a sample Chain of Title based on a hypothetical screenplay for an indie film.

Distribution deliverables consist of legal documents and physical items needed to distribute and market the film in each sold territory, in each format and on each platform.

A sales agent or producer often coordinates this responsibility, beginning with a Master Delivery Schedule. The producer and the distributor negotiate who will pay for the requirements. Some usual deliverables include:

* Audio output files up to 10 channels, and:
  - Commentary (DVD standard); and
  - Closed captioning/subtitles;
* "Behind-the-scenes" or "making of" or documentary footage;
* Chain of title and other legal documents, including a Certificate of Origin;

- Digital Cinema Package ("DCP") for each market and rights level (i.e., dubbed, foreign language subtitles, etc.);
- Dialogue continuity transcript (used for translations in foreign territories);
- DVD extras (interview footage, outtakes, audio commentary, casting tapes, etc.);
- Electronic Press Kit ("EPK");
- Errors & Omission ("E&O") Insurance;
- Film HDCam or digital files, and 35mm prints for non-digital theaters;
- Key art for ads and posters (in separated layers, important for foreign markets);
- Marketing print materials;
- MPAA ratings and other information;
- Premiere footage;
- Press package with production notes, press clippings, etc.;
- Social media platforms;
- Still on-set photographs (at least 100 to 200 high-quality photos);
- Theatrical trailer and TV commercials, if available; and
- Anything else to help market the film.

Producers should organize a deliverables binder with chain of title documents, contracts, and index. Physical materials should track the Master Deliverables Schedule.

After the producer finances, develops, produces and distributes her film, what should be done next? The next Chapter offers suggested strategies to build and continue the momentum for subsequent projects.

22.

WHAT'S NEXT?

What independent filmmaker has not dreamed of making a low-budget movie that achieves huge profits and return on investment from worldwide revenues on all platforms?

Consider the budgets, box office and returns on investment of films like *Clerks, El Mariachi, Night of the Living Dead* and *The Blair Witch Project.*

Table 22 compares and contrasts public financial information about these films.

TABLE 22 Select Indie Film Budgets, Box Office & Rate of Return				
Indie Film Title	Clerks	El Mariachi	Night of the Living Dead	The Blair Witch Project
Rate of Return	11,429%	28,571%	614,035%	416,667%
Budget (approx.)	$28,000	$7,000	$114,000	$60,000
Box Office (approx.)	$3.2 million	$2 million	$700 million	$250 million

As seen in Table 22, budgets of these indie films ranged from $7,000 to $114,000. Box office receipts were from $2 to $700 million, and the return on investment ranged from over 11,000 times to over 614,000 times.

There is no reason why a low-budget indie producer cannot achieve similar success, though producers always want larger budgets. A primary goal of indie producers is to make a new film just after wrapping one. To do so, financiers of the film must be repaid timely.

Repayment is more likely with indie films surrounded by buzz that screen at one or more important festivals and end up with strong distribution. But outstanding unknown films can make money if they are backed by a solid, creative "wow" marketing and promotion plan.

Numerous other books exist that provide information on creating film marketing plans, trailers, EPK's, social media campaigns and print materials. This book concentrates on how to raise funds for, or lower, the budget. But researching and creating such a marketing plan is crucial to a film's success.

Successful producers today must identify the target market for their film before they even start to raise money. Knowing potential buyers for a film before fundraising is the key to a strong marketing and promotional plan before, during and after production.

This strategy also allows producers to jump ahead of competitors, generate buzz and optimize many opportunities to sell their films.

What producer has not envisioned herself on the red carpet at a major film festival for the premiere of her film? This dream occurs often for many producers and filmmakers. More and more independent filmmakers are "discovered" and their films screened (and sometimes pre-sold) at prestigious festivals known for indie features.

After a film is produced, the marketing plan may result in a sale of all rights, licensing in some territories, few sales or none at all.

At wrap, producers should conduct a post-mortem to learn from mistakes and use them to propel forward on the next project. Follow-up communications should be sent to everyone who assisted with the film, including F&F, donors, lenders, investors, cast and crew, keeping them updated of the film's status and repaying all loans, investments and deferrals.

SUMMARY

Now it is time to review the 50 Ways you learned to make or reduce your budget using these tools, concepts and methods.

This book described different legal entities for production companies, such as limited liability companies, partnerships, corporations, sole proprietorships and fictitious businesses using a DBA name. You learned information to consider in hiring an entertainment attorney for a production. Explanations were given of how to obtain rights to screenplays, books and other types of literary material using options, work-for-hire agreements, and book-to-film adaptation agreements.

You learned the importance of copyrights, rights ownership and transfers and how to protect and register creative works with the U.S. Copyright Office. Information was also given on alternative dispute resolution methods to resolve infringement claims. Types of film marketing professionals and common distribution deals were explained as well.

The 50 Ways to obtain film financing offer multiple opportunities open to all passionate, committed filmmakers and producers. These Ways include investing your own skin in the game, using donations and grants, maximizing products and services to your advantage, coordinating team deferral efforts, being smart about locations, accessing incentives and rebates, maximizing tax credits, pre-sales, debt, crowdfunding (non-equity and equity) and private placement exemptions from securities registration to sell equity interests in a film.

The Forms Bank provides a Checklist of all of the 50 Ways and other crucial production information, as well as a sample Chain of Title.

Now you have the tools, skills and 50 Ways to make your film budget dream a reality. Use one or more Ways to get the Golden Goose, not a goose egg, for your budget.

Devise your plan, course-correct and modify your strategy as needed. Then go for it!

Happy film financing!

INDEX

A

Acquisition, 34, 189, 205, 206
Adaptation, see Book-to-film adaptation
Advances, Tax Credit, see Tax Credit Advances
Agent, 91, 92, 100, 122, 139, 142, 143, 193, 203, 205, 207, 213
Agent, Fiscal, 91, 92, 100; see also Sponsor, Fiscal
Agreement, 15, 23, 31, 33-35, 38-46, 51, 54, 55, 93, 112, 115, 117, 121, 122, 127, 128, 184, 203, 205, 206, 212; see also Contract
Alternative Dispute Resolution (ADR), 15, 33, 53, 56, 212
Angel, 85, 87, 145
Assignment, 38, 45, 46, 149, 186, 204, 205
Attorney, Entertainment, 29, 30, 32, 34-36, 142, 211
Attorney, Securities, 72, 178
Audit, 34, 136, 137, 161, 171

B

Back-end, 115-117, 119, 124, 154, 185-189; see also Profit Participation
Bond, 35, 73, 78, 79, 147, 151, 183
Book-to-film adaptation, 34, 45, 212, 213
Budget, 11,15, 31, 35, 36, 39, 59, 65, 71-73, 78, 85, 87, 88, 97, (continued)
Budget (continued), 104-106, 109, 110, 112-120, 123-125, 127-134, 137-139, 144, 146, 147, 152, 154, 155, 160-163, 180, 183, 184, 188 189, 208, 209-212

C

California Exemption, 15, 71, 176, 178, 213, 216
Chain of Title, 203-208, 212, 226
Collateral, 74, 147, 140 148, 150-153, 155, 159, 185, 201
Contract, 21, 33-35, 39, 40, 43, 44, 46, 54, 61, 62, 65, 93, 116, 120, 138, 143, 150, 185, 186, 195, 208; see also Agreement
Copyright, 15, 37, 38, 40, 41, 43-54, 58, 65, 200, 204, 212
Corporation, 20-23, 26, 28, 88, 91, 96, 98, 99, 137, 138, 148, 165, 176, 178, 211
Credit Line, see Line of Credit
Crowdfunding, Equity, see Regulation Crowdfunding
Crowdfunding, Non-equity, 15, 85, 94, 212

D

Debt, 15, 21, 23, 24, 26-28, 72, 82, 83, 119, 124,136, 144-155, 157, 185, 186, 188
Deferral, 15, 116, 117, 119-124, 136, 145, 186, 188, 189
Deliverables, 16, 203, 207, 208

Discount, 52, 63, 80, 110, 112, 113, 123, 126-128, 137, 138, 161, 162
Distribution, 13, 16, 41, 57, 65, 76, 117, 142-144, 150, 153-155, 184-186, 193-202, 205-207, 210, 212
Distributor, 56, 59, 60, 62-66, 75, 105, 107, 111, 139, 141, 142, 146, 153, 154, 189, 194-199, 201-203, 205, 207
Donation, 15, 81, 85, 88, 89, 91, 92, 94, 96, 103, 108, 110, 123, 145, 147, 164, 212
Donor, 85-91, 94-96, 164, 211

E
EIN, 27
Electronic Press Kit (EPK), 153, 207, 210
Equity, 12, 13, 15, 71, 72, 73, 76, 77, 80, 82, 83, 85, 87, 94, 124, 147, 149, 156, 162-165, 167, 176-180, 183, 185-189
Equity Crowdfunding, see Regulation (Equity) Crowdfunding
Errors & Omissions (E&O), 207; see also Insurance
Exemption, Registration, 12, 15, 27, 71, 72, 163-166, 173, 176-180
Exemption, Tax, 129-131, 133-135

F
F&F, see Friends & Family
Film Commissioner, 126
Film Festival, 14, 64, 142, 153, 195, 211, 219
Film Financing, 11-13, 15, 16, 29, 72, 73, (continued)

Film Financing (continued), 81, 84, 85, 94, 95, 97, 132, 135, 138-140, 144, 147-150, 152, 155,156, 159, 160, 162-165, 176, 178, 180, 184, 201, 212
Financing, see Film Financing; see Debt
FINRA, 165, 169, 170
Fixed, Copyright; 47, 51; see also Tangible Medium; see also Copyright
Four-wall, 154, 195; see also Distribution; see also Percentage Deal
Free, 52, 56, 57, 74, 82, 89, 90, 97, 103-106, 108-111, 112, 116, 126, 127–129, 135, 149, 159, 162, 219, 230
Friends & Family (F&F), 85-87

G
Gap Financing, 147, 150, 152; see also Super-Gap Financing; see also Mezzanine Financing
Grant, Financial, 87, 89, 92-94, 96-102
Guarantee, Foreign, see Minimum Guarantee (MG)

I
Incentive, 15, 126, 129-131, 134, 135, 147, 149, 160, 162, 212; see also Tax Credit
Infringement, 51, 212
Insurance, 73, 79, 80, 107, 112, 127, 128, 207
Intrastate Exemption, 179

J

Jurisdiction, 23, 25, 31, 32, 34, 128-138, 149, 160-162; see also Location

L

Legal Structure, 201
Lender, 15, 75, 82, 139, 146-156, 161, 162, 184-188, 201, 211
License, Business, 28
License, Copyright, 39, 40, 42, 61, 66, 204; see also Option Exercise
License, Law, 30, 31
Limited Liability Company (LLC), 23, 27, 143, 165
Limited Partnership, 179
Literary Work, 26, 150, 157
Litigation, 86; see also Alternative Dispute Resolution (ADR)
Line of Credit, 82, 156-159
Literary Material, 15, 37, 39, 40, 44, 199, 212
Litigation, 15, 26, 32, 33, 36, 53, 58
Location, Film, 15, 28, 41, 56, 72, 109, 125-134, 136, 137, 160, 162, 205, 212
Lodging Tax Rebate, 130

M

Marketing, 14, 58, 59, 64, 65, 89, 107, 133, 136, 143, 144, 155, 199, 200, 208, 210-212
Mezzanine Financing, 147, 150-152, 155: see also Debt
Minimum Guarantee (MG), 140

N

Negative Pick-up, 201

O

Option, 13, 15, 25, 34, 38-42, 44,45, 51, 204, 205
Option and Acquisition, 38, 39, 52
Option Exercise, 39-42
Option Extension, 41, 42

P

Paper Form Copyright, 52
Partnership, 20, 23, 26, 213
Percentage Deal, 195; see also Four-wall; see also Distribution
Pre-sale, 139-142, 198, 212
Prints and Advertising (P&A), 153, 196
Producers Guild of America (PGA), 218
Producers Representative, 35, 36, 59-63, 66, 193
Product Integration, 103, 106, 107, 145
Product Placement, 103, 105, 106
Production Counsel, 29, 46, 65; see also Attorney, Entertainment
Profit Participation, 115, 117, 124, 188; see also Back-end

R

Real estate, 26, 82, 83, 143, 147, 204
Rebate, Lodging Tax, 130
Rebate, Sales Tax, 131, 132

Registration, see Exemption
Regulation (Equity)
Crowdfunding, 15, 71, 163-176, 186
Rent-a-Distributor/Rent-a-Studio, 196, 201, 202; see also Distribution; see also Four-wall
Retirement Fund, 73, 83, 84
Reversion/Reversionary Right, 40, 203, 204
Rule 147, see Intrastate Exemption
Rule 147A, see Intrastate Exemption
Rule 1001; see California Exemption

S

SAG-AFTRA, 116, 121
Sale, of copyright, see Assignment
Sale, of exclusive right, see Assignment; see License
Sale, Tax Credit, see Tax Credit Sale
Sales Agent, 60, 63, 65, 66, 67, 139, 142-144, 193, 203, 205, 207
Sales Estimates, 139, 140
Sales Tax Rebate, 131, 132
Section 3(a)(11), see Intrastate Offering Exemption
Security/Securities, 12, 13, 15, 36, 71, 72, 78, 87, 94, 128, 149, 153, 162-166, 168, 170-180, 186, 212
Securities & Exchange Commission, 71, 163
Senior Debt, 147-150, 152, 154, 155, 185; see also Debt
Skin in the Game, 15, 73, 74, 76, 79-84, 86, 118
Slate financing, 148, 149, 155, 156
Sole proprietor, 19, 20, 24-26, 211
Sponsor, Fiscal, 85, 91-94, 100, 213; see also Agent, Fiscal
Super-Gap Financing, 147, 150, 152; see also Gap Financing; see also Mezzanine Financing
Statutory damages, 51

T

Tangible Medium of Expression, 47-52; see also Copyright, Fixed
Tax Credit Advance, 159, 161
Tax Credit Rebate, 135
Tax Credit Sale, 34, 136, 138
Taxes, 23, 28, 84, 129-135, 183, 184
Television Sales Agent, 59, 63, 66
Territories, Foreign or International, 65, 66, 138-141, 150, 151, 152, 154, 206, 207, 211
Theatrical Release, 64, 76, 163, 194, 195; see also Distribution

U

U.S. Copyright Office (USCO), 51, 52, 212

W

World Intellectual Property Organization (WIPO), 53, 58

APPENDIX

A. ENTERTAINMENT ASSOCIATIONS, GUILDS & ORGANIZATIONS

1. Academy of Motion Picture Arts & Sciences: www.oscars.org
2. Academy of Television Arts & Sciences: see Television Academy
3. Alliance of Motion Picture and Television Producers: www.amptp.org
4. Alliance of Women Directors: www.allianceofwomendirectors.org
5. Alliance for Women Sound Composers: www.theawfc.com
6. American Society of Cinematographers: www.theasc.org
7. Animation Guild: www.animationguild.org
8. Assoc. of Film Commissioners Intl: www.afci.org
9. Assoc. of Independent Commercial Producers: www.aicp.com
10. Assoc. of Independent Video & Filmmakers: www.aivf.org
11. Assoc. of Talent Agents: www.agentassociation.com
12. Casting Society of America: www.castingsociety.com
13. Directors Guild of America: www.dga.org
14. Film Fatales: www.filmfatales.org
15. Filmmakers Alliance: FilmmakersAlliance.org
16. Geena Davis Institute on Gender & Media: www.seejane.org
17. Independent Film & Television Alliance: www.IFTAonline.org
18. International Documentary Assoc.: www.documentary.org
19. International Federation of Film Producers Association: www.fiapf.org
20. Location Managers Guild Intl: www.locationmanagers.org
21. Motion Picture Assoc. of America: www.mpaa.org

22. Music Video Production Assoc.: www.mvpa.com
23. National Association of Broadcasters: www.nab.org
24. National Association of Theater Owners: www.natoonline.org
25. National Film Preservation Foundation: www.filmpreservation.org
26. National Music Publishers Assoc.: nmpa.org
27. New York Women in Film & Television: www.nywift.org
28. Producers Guild of America: www.producersguild.org
29. SAG-AFTRA: www.sagaftra.org
30. Set Decorator's Society of America: www.setdecorators.org
31. Sundance Institute: www.sundance.org
32. Television Academy: www.emmys.org
33. Television Academy/Students: www.emmys.org/membership/student
34. The Latin Recording Academy: miembros.latingrammy.com/es/join/voting
35. The Recording Academy: www.grammypro.com
36. The Recording Academy/Students: www.grammy.org/recording-academy/grammy-u
37. University Film & Video Assoc.: www.ufva.org
38. Women in Film: www.womeninfilm.org
39. Women in Film & Video of Washington, D.C.: wifv.org
40. Writers Guild of America: www.wga.org

B. FILM PUBLICATIONS, BLOGS & WEBSITES

41. *Beyond Cinema*: www.afci.org/beyond-cinema
42. Box Office Mojo: www.boxofficemojo.com
43. *Cineaste*: www.cineaste.com
44. *Cinema Editor Magazine*: americancinemaeditors.org/cinemaeditor
45. *Creative Screenwriting*: www.creativescreenwriting.com
46. *Deadline*: www.deadline.com
47. *Emmy® Magazine*: www.emmys.com

FINANCING INDEPENDENT FILMS | 221

48. *Fade In Magazine*: www.fadeinonline.com
49. *Film Comment*: www.filmcomment.com
50. Film Festivals Online: www.filmfestivals.com
51. Film Festivals Online Free Submission Platform: www.filmfestivals.com/en/blog/festivalexpress
52. *Film Independent*: www.filmindependent.org
53. *Filmmaker Magazine*: www.filmmakermagazine.com
54. *Grammy Magazine*: www.grammy.com/photos/read-grammy-magazine
55. *Hollywood Reporter*: www.hollywoodreporter.com
56. *Hollywood Scriptwriter Magazine*: www.hollywoodscriptwriter.com
57. *Indiewire*: www.indiewire.com
58. *Indie Slate*: www.indieslate.dom
59. *InkTip Magazine*: www.inktip.com
60. Internet Movie Database: www.imdb.com
61. Internet Movie Database Pro Version: www.imdbpro.com
62. *Movie Maker Magazine*: www.moviemaker.com
63. Movie Web: www.movieweb.com
64. No Film School: www.nofilmschool.com
65. *P3 Update Magazine*: www. p3update.com
66. *Produced By Magazine*: www.producersguild.org
67. ProductionHUB: www.production hub.com
68. *Production Weekly*: www.productionweekly. com
69. Raindance: www.raindance.org/blog
70. *Screen*: www.screenmag.com
71. Screen Daily: www.screendaily.com
72. *Screen International*: www.screeninternational magazine. com
73. *Script Magazine*: www.scriptmag.com
74. Social media platform for filmmakers & festivals: www. Fest21.com
75. *The Field Guide to Sponsored Films*, by Rick Prelinger: www. filmpreservation.org/userfiles/image/PDFs/sponsored.pdf
76. *The Independent Magazine*: www.independent-magazine.org/
77. The Numbers: www.the-numbers.com

78. *Variety*: www.variety.com
79. *Video Watchdog*: www.videowatchdog.com

C. GRANT RESOURCES

80. California Humanities: www.calhum.org
81. Catapult Film Fund: www.catapultfilmfund.org
82. Center for Asian-American Media (CAAM): www.caamedia.org
83. Chicago Filmmakers: www.chicagofilmmakers.org
84. Derek Freese Film Fund: www.derekfreesefilm.org
85. The Documentary Company: www.documentarycompany.com
86. Film Independent: www.filmindependent.org
87. The Filmmaker Fund: www.filmmakerfund.com
88. Filmmakers Without Borders: filmmakerswithoutborders.org
89. The Fledgling Fund: www.thefledglingfund.org
90. Ford Foundation: www.fordfoundation.org
91. Fork Film Fund: www.forkfilms.net
92. Gucci Tribeca Documentary Fund: www.tribecafilminstitute.org
93. Hartley Film Foundation: hartleyfoundation.org
94. Impact Partners Film Fund: www.impactpartnersfilm.com
95. Independent Filmmaker Project (IFP): www.ifp.org
96. International Documentary Association: www.ida.org
97. ITVS: www.itvs.org
98. Latino Public Broadcasting: www.lphb.org
99. National Endowment for the Arts: ww.nea.gov
100. National Endowment for the Humanities: www.neh.gov
101. Nextpix/Firstpix Crowdfunding Program: www.nextpix.com
102. Pacific Pioneer Fund: www.pacificpioneerfund.com
103. Panavision's New Filmmaker Program: www.panavision.com/new-filmmaker-program
104. PBS/Corporation for Public Broadcasting: www.cpb.org/grants

FINANCING INDEPENDENT FILMS | 223

105. Public Broadcasting Service Documentary Funding Resources: www.pbs.org/pov/filmmakers/resources/documentary-funding.php
106. Redford Center: www.redfordcenter.org
107. Sundance Institute: www.sundance.org
108. Vision Maker Media: www.visionmakermedia.org
109. Women in Film Finishing Fund: www.womeninfilm.org/film-finishing-fund
110. Women Make Movies (Fiscal Sponsorship): www.wmm.com

D. U.S. GOVERNMENT OFFICES

112. U.S. Copyright Office: www.copyright.gov
113. U.S. Patent & Trademark Office: www.uspto.gov
114. U.S. Securities & Exchange Comm.: www.sec.gov
115. U.S. Small Business Administration: www.sba.gov

E. STATE SECRETARY OF STATE OFFICES

116. Alabama: www.sos.state.al.us
117. Alabama: sos.alabama.gov
118. Alaska: www.commerce.alaska.gov
119. Arizona: www.azcc.gov
120. Arkansas: www.sos.arkansas.gov
121. California: www.ss.ca.gov
122. Colorado: www.sos.state.co.us
123. Connecticut: www.ct.gov/sots
124. Delaware: www.corp.delaware.gov
125. District of Columbia: dcra.dc.gov
126. Florida: dos.myflorida.com
127. Georgia: sos.ga.gov
128. Hawaii: portal.ehawaii.gov
129. Idaho: www.sos.idaho.gov
130. Illinois: ilsos.com
131. Indiana: www.in.gov/sos
132. Iowa: sos.iowa.gov
133. Kansas: www.kssos.org
134. Kentucky: sos.ky.gov
135. Louisiana: www.sos.la.gov
136. Maine: www.state.me.us/sos

137. Maryland: www.sos.state.md.us
138. Massachusetts: www.sec.state.ma.us
139. Michigan: www.michigan.gov/lara (Licensing/Regulatory Affairs)
140. Minnesota: www.sos.state.mn.us
141. Mississippi: www.sos.ms.gov
142. Missouri: www.sos.mo.gov
143. Montana: www.sos.mt.gov
144. Nebraska: www.sos.ne.gov
145. Nevada: www.nvsos.gov
146. New Hampshire: sos.nh.gov
147. New Jersey: www.nj.gov/njbusiness
148. New Mexico: www.sos.state.nm.us
149. New York: www.dos.ny.gov
150. North Carolina: www.sosnc.gov
151. North Dakota: sos.nd.gov
152. Ohio: www.sos.state.oh.us
153. Oklahoma: sos.ok.gov
154. Oregon: sos.oregon.gov
155. Pennsylvania: www.dos.pa.gov
156. Rhode Island: sos.ri.gov
157. South Carolina: www.scsos.com
158. South Dakota: sdsos.gov
159. Tennessee: sos.tn.gov
160. Texas: www.sos.state.tx.us
161. Utah: www.utah.gov/government/secretary-of-state.html
162. Vermont: www.sec.state.vt.us
163. Virginia: www.virginia.gov/Business/Business-One-Stop
164. Washington: www.sos.wa.gov
165. West Virginia: www.sos.wv.gov
166. Wisconsin: www.wdfi.org
167. Wyoming: soswy.state.wy.us

FORMS BANK

A. FILM FINANCING CHECKLIST

Consider this checklist of the 50 Ways and other elements from this book before seeking financing for an independent feature film.

NO.	DESCRIPTION	DATE DONE	NOTES
1	Legal Structure		
2	Legal & Marketing Pros		
3	Acquire Literary Material		
4	Copyright		
5	Work-for-Hire Agreements		
6	ADR		
7	Cash		
8	Credit Cards		
9	Stocks & Bonds		
10	Insurance		
11	Vehicle		
12	Retirement		
13	Real Estate		
14	F&F		
15	Angels		
16	Donors		
17	Sponsors & Agents		
18	Crowdfunding: Non-Equity		

19	Grants		
20	Products 1		
21	Products 2		
22	Products 3		
23	Services 1		
24	Services 2		
25	Equipment 1		
26	Equipment 2		
27	Deferrals 1		
28	Deferrals 2		
29	Deferrals 3		
30	Deferrals 4		
31	Deferrals 5		
32	Back-end		
33	Banks		
34	Mezzanine		
35	Gap/Super-Gap		
36	Wrap		
37	Line of Credit		
38	P&A		
39	Tax Credit Advances		
40	Locations 1		
41	Locations 2		
42	Rebates 1		
43	Waivers 1		
44	Rebates 2		

FINANCING INDEPENDENT FILMS | 227

45	Waivers 2		
46	Tax Credit Rebates		
47	Tax Credit Sales		
48	Sales Agents		
49	Domestic Distribution 1		
50	Domestic Distribution 2		
51	International Distribution 1		
52	International Distribution 2		
53	Foreign Estimates		
54	Foreign Pre-Sales		
55	Festival Sales		
56	Crowdfunding: Equity		
57	CA Exemption		
58	Production Accountant		
59	Tax Credit Audit		
60	Marketing & Social Media		
61	Film Festivals		
62	Waterfall: P&A		
63	Waterfall: Debt		
64	Waterfall: Deferrals		
65	Waterfall: Equity		
66	Waterfall: Back-End		
67	Waterfall: Producer Share		
68	Post-Mortem		
69	Repeat for next film		

B. SAMPLE CHAIN OF TITLE

A sample chain of title document is provided for the following hypothetical screenplay situation:

Filmmaker Alicia Billings formed her own production company, Alicia in Wonderfilms, Inc. on February 20, 2020.

Screenwriter Charlie Durham completed and registered his screenplay entitled "Now, Not Later" for copyright with the U.S. Copyright Office ("USCO") on March 2, 2020. He received Certificate of Registration number PA-1-234-567 from the USCO, effective as of that date.

On September 3, 2020, Charlie Durham and Alicia in Wonderfilms, Inc. executed an option and acquisition agreement for Durham's screenplay entitled "Now, Not Later."

Alicia in Wonderfilms, Inc. exercised the option and purchased the screenplay "Now, Not Later" from Charlie Durham on October 1, 2020. The same day, the parties executed an assignment agreement from Durham to Alicia in Wonderfilms, Inc. for the screenplay. Also on that date, the company registered the assignment and received Certificate of Registration number PA-2-345-678. At this point, the film has not been produced yet.

Since that time, no other transactions have occurred affecting ownership right, title and interest to the screenplay. The following sample Chain of Title chart details these transactions in a commonly-accepted format.

CAVEAT: This sample chart is provided for educational purposes only, is not legal advice and may not be relied upon as such. Consult an entertainment lawyer for a chain of title for a specific screenplay.

"NOW, NOT LATER"
SCREENPLAY CHAIN OF TITLE
As of October 1, 2020

1. <u>2 March 2020</u>, United States Copyright Office registration (2 March 2020) (Registration No. PA-1-234-567) by Charlie Durham of original screenplay entitled "Now, Not Later," written by Charlie Durham.

2. <u>3 September 2020</u>, Option and acquisition agreement of screenplay entitled "Now, Not Later," written by Charlie Durham, optioned by Alicia in Wonderfilms, Inc. from Charlie Durham.

3. <u>1 October 2020</u>, Assignment agreement from Charlie Durham to Alicia in Wonderfilms, Inc. of screenplay entitled "Now, Not Later."

4. <u>1 October 2020</u>, United States Copyright Office registration (1 October 2020) (Registration no. PA-2-345-678) of assignment of copyright from Charlie Durham to Alicia in Wonderfilms, Inc. of screenplay entitled "Now, Not Later."

NOTE: Add to this chain any subsequent agreements affecting ownership rights in and to the screenplay as well as the film when it is produced.

ABOUT THE AUTHOR
M. M. Le BLANC

The author M. M. Le Blanc, JD, MBA, is a veteran Hollywood film & television studio executive and international entertainment attorney previously in-house at Fox, Disney/ABC, Universal/Canal+, MGM Studios/United Artists and other media companies.

Le Blanc previously worked for the Securities and Exchange Commission in the Enforcement Division. Subsequently, Le Blanc raised substantial investor financing as a licensed broker-dealer and as an issuer.

The author has been involved in countless film and television productions and obtained certifications for over a Billion Dollars of state film and TV tax credits. Le Blanc also advised governors, legislatures and economic offices in multiple states on drafting tax credit and entertainment legislation, including Coogan's Law, and consulted in Europe and Asia.

Le Blanc is the multi-award-winning author of twenty novels and non-fiction books, and has authored dozens of articles and columns published in entertainment, law and business journals in the USA, Europe and Asia.

The author's academic experience includes as Academic Dean, Department Chair and Professor of Finance, Entertainment Law, Entertainment Business and Intellectual Property, at film, law and business schools and universities in the USA and Europe.

Le Blanc is a frequently-invited guest speaker and panelist at film festivals, film and television markets and entertainment industry conferences throughout the world on topics of entertainment law and finance.

Le Blanc was selected one of the "Top Ten Young Working Women in America" and is a member of the Academy of Television Arts & Sciences (TV Academy) in Los Angeles.

Contact the Author
Email: **bizentinepress@gmail.com**

Contact the Publisher
Email: **bizentinepress@gmail.com**

NOTES

www.ingramcontent.com/pod-product-compliance
Lightning Source LLC
Chambersburg PA
CBHW072002110526
44592CB00012B/1183